WEIRD HABERDASHERY

After spotting a 25-year-old man walk
Baltimore street, a police officer stopp
twenty-one live pigeons and five dead ones stuffed in his
pants. The officer reported that the man "looked like
the Michelin tire ad."

THE WORLD AS HE SEES IT

In revenge for England's closing of the Libyan embassy
in London, Col. Muammar el-Qadafi ordered that England be deleted from all Libyan maps in the mid-1980s.
In its place was put a new arm of the North Sea, bordered by Scotland and Wales.

FETISHES ON PARADE

A Burbank, California, husband and wife returned home
from a skiing weekend to find a 45-year-old man occupying their house, wearing her lingerie. He had rearranged furniture, emptied perfume bottles, thrown away
food, and posted notes at various points about the house
about President Reagan and Sally Field.

FELONIOUS FOOD

London police investigating the death of 56-year-old Leslie Merry, who was fatally injured by a turnip thrown from
a passing car, said the attack was carried out by a gang
whose members toss vegetable at random at passersby.
Investigators noted that three months before Mary's death,
another man suffered stomach injuries when he was hit
by a cabbage.

MORE NEWS OF THE WEIRD

Chuck Shepherd
John J. Kohut
Roland Sweet

Illustrations by Drew Friedman

A PLUME BOOK

PLUME
Published by the Penguin Group
Penguin Books USA Inc., 375 Hudson Street,
New York, New York 10014, U.S.A.
Penguin Books Ltd, 27 Wrights Lane,
London W8 5TZ, England
Penguin Books Australia Ltd, Ringwood,
Victoria, Australia
Penguin Books Canada Ltd, 2801 John Street,
Markham, Ontario, Canada L3R 1B4
Penguin Books (N.Z.) Ltd, 182–190 Wairau Road,
Auckland 10, New Zealand

Penguin Books Ltd, Registered Offices:
Harmondsworth, Middlesex, England

First published by Plume, an imprint of New American Library, a division of
Penguin Books USA Inc.

First Printing, November, 1990
10 9 8 7 6 5 4 3 2 1

 REGISTERED TRADEMARK—MARCA REGISTRADA

Library of Congress Cataloging-in-Publication Data
Shepherd, Chuck.
    More news of the weird / Chuck Shepherd, John J. Kohut, Roland Sweet ; illustrations
by Drew Friedman.
        p.   cm.
    "A Plume book."
    ISBN 0-452-26545-2
    1. United States—History, Local—Anecdotes. 2. Curiosities and wonders—United States—
Anecdotes.   I. Kohut, John J.   II. Sweet, Roland.   III. Title.
E179.S548   1990
973—dc20
                                                                                    90-39975
                                                                                    CIP

PRINTED IN THE UNITED STATES OF AMERICA
Set in Souvenir
Designed by Leonard Telesca

Contents

Acknowledgments

We wish to express our gratitude to everyone who read our first book and sent us their favorite clippings. We enjoyed them all.

For these two books, we have had access to large numbers of clippings from the collections of our peers T. S. Child, Jonathan Ginsburg, Bill Golden, Eugene Grealish, Everett Long, and Tony Tellier.

We also would like to thank those people who made a special contribution to this second volume of weird news. They are:

Jim White, Jamie Moore, Bill Harris, John Orr, Lisa Reed, Roxanne Scott, Chris DeVries, Rex Wingerter, Kerry Loring, Heidi Bunes, David Landsidle, Peter Favini, Mr. Eagen's, Susan Scheer, Julian Scheer, Magdalen Kohut, Joe Kohut, Jake Geesing, and, especially, Melissa Walker.

Stephen C. Lee, Rebecca Kuenstler, Michael Reade, Maurine Taylor, Brian Emrich, Dave Embry, and John Fox.

Loren Coleman, Gary Larson, Seth Morris, Jan Harold Brunvand, and Annette Grundy.

Also Mike Greenstein, Steve Moss, Margaret Engle, L. Richard "Rick" Mariani, Kihm Winship, John R. Kupferer, and Theodora Tilton.

Other immortal contemporary weird clippers include Kenneth Anger, Gaal Shepherd Crowl, Sam Gaines, Marilyn Green, Chuck Jones, Myra Linden, Dale Lowdermilk, Ray Nelke (ret.), the irrepressible Chip Rogers, Jim Sweeney, and Christine Van Lenten.

Nearly immortal are Ed Aderer, Linda Anderson, Russell Ash,

Jenny Beatty, Randle Brashear, Anne Chavré, Linda Cunningham, Tim Dorr, Ernie Englander, Paul Evans, Ellen Haug, Dave Hotaling, Dorothy John, Paul R. Jones, Jim Kane, Rich Kline, Mike Lewyn, Diane Marcus, Bill Martin, Bob Maslow, David Menconi, Matt Mirapaul, John Morgan, Ken Nahigian, Tom Nelson, Marci Novak, John Pell, Linda Phillips, Yvonne Pover, Barbara Kate Repa, Jay Russell, C. C. Shepherd, J. B. Smetana, Debby Stirling, Pat Washburn, Bill Wauters, Elaine Weiss, Tracy Westen, Brian Wilson, Elliot Woodward, and Susan Zurcher.

Also very helpful were Gary Abbott, Irwin Arieff, Jean Arnold, Steve Banister, Jerry Benedict, Jeff Brandt, Dan Brennan, Margo Brown, Trapper Byrne, Burr Carrington, Terry Carter, Jon Choy, Stephanie Clipper, Ron Cotterill, René Couture, Virginia Crawford, Ed Cress, Nancy Debevoise, Mark DelMaramo, Chris Dodge, Peter Doherty, George Duquesnel, Kristi Edon, Geoffrey Egan, Bob Eland, Dave Elgin, Jamie Elvebak, Joe Ferrandino, Annette Friedman, Brien Galvin, Gail Gleeson, Leslie Goodman-Malamuth, Barbara Gudenius, Eric Haines, Robert Haines, Jeff Halperin, Dennis Hartzell, Libby Hatch, Dr. Steven Hill, Jim Hogan, Alex Hooke, Jackie Howell, Thomas Izaguirre, Bob Jones, Scott Kelley, Jane Kochersperger, Frederick Kopec, Gene Kuhn, Scott Langill, Dr. Robert Lacy, Sylvia Lee, Linda Lemoine, Howard Lenard, J. Michael Lenninger, Peggy Ligon, Fred Lipton, Fred McChesney, Ross MacKenzie, Steve Magnuson, Paul Maiorana, Bob Manley, Gail Martin, Peter Michaels, Paul Miller, Carol Moore, Terry Murphy, Amanda Ford Neal, Bill Nelson, Stafford Ordahl, Matt Paust, John Peterson, Paul Peterson, Edward O. Phillips, Jerome Pohlen, Anthony Powell, Sam Randlett, Dave Raney, Rollo Rayjaway, Harry Roach, Joni Sager, Stan Saplin, Joe Schwind, Ronald Semone, Amy Sheon, Ruby Shepherd, Wes Simpson, Richard Siskind, Michael K. Smith, Martin Avery Snyder, Allan Spitzer, Milford Sprecher, Dave Stein, Maurice Suhre, Susie Thompson, Marty Turnauer, Elyse Versé, Earl Vickers, John Vogl, Mike Vogl, Kevin Walsh, Will Ward, Debbie Weeter, Whitney Whitmire, Doug Wilson, Tim Wyatt, and Karen Youngreen.

MORE NEWS
OF THE
WEIRD

Introduction

This second volume of *News of the Weird* was inevitable from the moment we began sorting through our classic clippings to choose the ones for the first volume. There's just too much good stuff for one book, we agreed. Indeed, the only way we could keep it to the five hundred items the publisher wanted instead of turning it into the *Encyclopedia Weirdica* was to set aside hundreds of weird news items every bit as good as the stuff we used. To this sequel file—or "pile," as it quickly became—we added the best of our current clippings.

Then *News of the Weird* appeared. We were totally unprepared for the deluge of clippings from the readers. They sent in not just the few we hoped for but sometimes entire collections. We were overjoyed to find some old favorites and not a few new ones.

From contemplating these clippings, we've deduced one pertinent fact about who collects weird news. It's everybody.

The weird news community is universal. Everybody notices news stories odd enough to clip and save. We've seen enough bulletin boards and gotten enough mail to confirm our observation.

We may go at it more zealously than most people (though by no means all), but we're astonished at how every mention of the book brought more mail. At book parties and signings, people would bring clippings to show us, some yellowed and a few laminated. We did all together fifty radio interviews. John and Roland appeared on Larry King's TV call-in show. In almost every case, people called in to share their weird news. Our favorite was the guy who was just passing through town when he happened to tune in to the station where we were talking about weird news. He pulled off the road to get to a pay phone and called the station to read a clipping he carried in his wallet that had been given him by his father, who clipped it twenty years ago.

Then Chuck was written up in *The Atlantic*. You'd expect a few of that august journal's readers to have clipped a few oddities over the years and actually take the time to send them in, but who'd have anticipated better than a thousand people unleashing a torrent. Not just one or two items in a No. 10 envelope, but thick bubble-pack mailers brimming with quality weird news.

John gets more requests than he can handle for his newsletter "The Caretakers of Earth." Pleas for Chuck's "View from the Ledge" have umptydrupled. His column "News of the Weird," distributed by Universal Press Syndicate, is now carried in nearly a hundred papers in cities and towns across America. Roland's column of weird news for AlterNet now appears under various guises in some fifteen alternative newsweeklies.

We all have been touched to receive clips from some of our longtime heroes and to hear from weird news compatriots who sent us their remarkable newsletters.

Thank you all for your weird news. Such an outpouring has turned us into America's Refrigerator Door, an informal weird news clearing house—an arrangement we'd be more than willing to formalize on receipt of a hefty grant.

What all of this boils down to is that this is one sequel that outdoes the original. Future volumes will be even better. We've already got enough gems picked out for the next one.

It's a labor of love, sure, but we also take our responsibility as advocates for the weird news community very seriously. We aren't three crackpots you'd wonder if should be allowed to have sharp scissors. We see ourselves as scholars of the genre. Weirdologists. With full tenure.

In this vein, at the back of this book, we have appended several essays based on our observations for those of you who react to this as more than just a collection of weird news and want to delve into the topic somewhat more academically. But you won't be tested on any of the material, and you get to read and enjoy the weird news first.

If by slim chance you weren't one of the thousands of people who responded to our first book by sharing your clippings with us, we repeat the invitation. Send any and all, with or without comments, to:

Strange News
P.O. Box 25682
Washington, D.C. 20007

We thank you.

CHUCK SHEPHERD
JOHN J. KOHUT
ROLAND SWEET

IN THE WRONG PLACE AT THE WRONG TIME

A 22-year-old man in Milwaukee called ahead to his cocaine supplier to make sure he was open and had a supply on hand, but his phone call went through just as the police entered to execute a search warrant on the dealer's premises. A police officer impersonating the dealer said he had "plenty" of stuff on hand, and the man and three friends were arrested as they later showed up at the dealer's house.

Two undocumented aliens were trying to slip into the U.S. near San Ysidro, California, when they had the misfortune of stumbling into the path of an office pentathlon event being staged by the U.S. Border Patrol. While some officers continued the endurance run, a couple dropped out and arrested the pair.

○

Patricia Spahic, 59, sitting in the third row during a Pittsburgh production of *Hamlet* in 1989, was cut on the head when Hamlet's dagger slipped out of his hand and sailed into the audience.

○

Joan Raeburn, 26, of West Harrison, Indiana, was traveling by car on a rural road near the Ohio state line in 1987 when she was the victim of a hit-and-run pilot, who grazed the roof of her car with his single-engine airplane and flew off into the night.

○

William Ashurst awoke one morning in the Los Angeles suburb of Duarte in the 1960s to find a 700-pound electric transformer in his bed, spewing "big flashes like lightning," he said. High winds had blown down a 30-foot-tall oak tree onto a utility pole, sending it through Ashurst's ceiling.

○

Edward Clark Wright, 42, of Dove Canyon, California, apparently received a bullet wound to the head while a passenger in a commuter plane that was landing at Fort Lauderdale, Florida, airport. The plane had been fired upon by someone on the ground for unknown reasons. He said he heard a popping noise and felt a bump on his head that was bleeding. A bullet hole was found in the plane.

○

A man was shot and killed while lying in his bed in his Austin, Texas, apartment in 1988 by the man downstairs, who had fired a loaded pistol up through the ceiling by accident.

○

A New York City undercover narcotics officer, testifying before a grand jury in 1989, glanced up from the witness stand toward the jury and recognized Anthony Eisenberg, a 23-year-old man he had been pursuing for nearly a month but could not find. Police said Eisenberg might have been crafty in sitting on the grand jury because he could then have learned the identities of over 100 undercover narcotics officers.

○

The following people reported being hit by various items:

Carlton Carroll, 5, was knocked unconscious in 1987 by a 250-pound brown-spotted ray that leapt from the water into his family's fishing boat.

Elmer Searle, 80, was knocked unconscious by a "flying dog" that had been propelled through the air after being struck by a car in Sacramento.

Lui Wai-kwong, 36, was injured when hit on the head by a two-pound turtle while walking to work in Hong Kong in 1987. The turtle apparently fell from a nearby high-rise building.

Fisherman Josaia Tusoba, 31, was severely wounded in his

boat 60 miles from Suva, Fiji, when a 3-foot-long sword-fish, apparently attracted by the sun reflecting on the boat, leapt from the ocean and speared him in the chest.

○

Biagio di Crescenzo, 23, smashed his car into a tree near Rome and was badly injured. After a motorist took him to a hospital, he was sent in an ambulance toward another hospital for further treatment, but the ambulance smashed into an oncoming car. A motorist took him to another hospital, where he was again dispatched in an ambulance for further treatment. That ambulance smashed into another car in a suburb of Rome, killing di Crescenzo.

○

Don Oestreich and Bernice Johnson, distracted by the colors of the fall foliage while boating on the Mississippi River in Minnesota, shot over a 40-foot dam and into the rushing overflow below, but were rescued by two fishermen.

WEIRD HABER-DASHERY

A man wearing a G-string, chaps, a shirt, and shoes—but no pants—was arrested in Los Angeles at 3 o'clock one morning while being led down a city sidewalk on a chain by another man. The man in the chaps was booked on suspicion of indecent exposure, but the man leading him by the chain was not arrested because there is no law against leading someone by a chain.

○

After spotting Thomas Waddell walking oddly down a Baltimore street with his pants bulging, police officer Ronald Pettie stopped the 25-year-old man and found twenty-one live pigeons and five dead ones stuffed in Waddell's pants. Pettie reported that Waddell "looked like the Michelin tire ad."

In 1981, the Hare Krishna sect purchased a mansion outside Paris that was once owned by eighteenth-century philosopher Jean-Jacques Rousseau. As a condition of the sale, members of the shaven-headed sect agreed to wear wigs so they wouldn't frighten the neighbors.

○

A Trenton woman coming out of a New Jersey National Bank branch was robbed of $91 in food stamps by a tall man wearing a black rubber suit and flippers who threatened to shoot her. The woman said she believed the threat because the man was carrying a long case that could have contained a speargun.

○

A woman wearing a hat with a large black feather and a low-cut dress with shrubbery tied to her waist tried to withdraw $90,000 she didn't have in her account from the Third National Bank in Nashville. When the teller wouldn't give her the money, the woman pulled a butcher knife from the shrubbery. Bank employee Mark Winn said that the woman "looked like a big tree."

○

A suspected narcotics dealer in Washington, D.C., was arrested as he sat in his parked car sipping Schlitz Malt Liquor, which used a bull in its advertising, by an undercover officer dressed as a bull. The rented costume used in the arrest was designed to embarrass the 31-year-old suspect, who police Sgt. John Kornutick said had given police "a lot of abuse" in the past.

○

The Fall River, Massachusetts, city council passed a measure banning snakes in public places after a pregnant constituent of Councilor Leo Pelletier was frightened by two men wearing live snakes as they walked down a busy street. Pelletier, who noted that people with pet boa constrictors often wrap them around their bodies when they take them out for air, said he had considered a leash law before deciding to propose a total ban.

○

In 1979 the Navy banned its polyester double-knit uniforms, worn since 1971, from the engine rooms of its surface ships after an officer aboard the destroyer *Manley* died of burns received when his uniform melted around him.

○

West Delaware High School in Manchester, Iowa, acted to curb students' rest-room breaks by requiring students on their way to the bathroom to wear toilet seats around their necks.

○

A Chinese footwear factory in Canton introduced fragrant shoes it claimed not only prevented sweating but also helped cure beriberi.

PEOPLE WHO WON'T TAKE NO FOR AN ANSWER

Margaret Hunter had been trying to get a driver's license for over twenty years by the early 1970s when yet another try failed because no one would lend her a car for the test. Her latest instructor had walked out the week before the test, saying Hunter wasn't ready. Previously, one instructor had leapt from her car during the test, screaming that riding with her was "suicide," and another flunked her because she made (on one test) seven false starts, ran a red light, and parallel-parked no closer than 3 feet from the curb.

○

Lung-cancer patient George Stickler, 59, couldn't wait until he was off pure-oxygen therapy before lighting up a cigarette at a Lafayette, Louisiana, hospital in 1988. The resulting fire gave Stickler second-degree burns and forced the evacuation of several other patients.

○

In a 1981 incident, as gunfire rang out in a Las Vegas casino when police scurried to catch some troublemakers, dozens of officers had to climb over casino customers, who had dropped to their knees but continued to feed the slot machines.

○

In 1978 Leonard Njuguna Muraya, a Kenyan exchange student at the University of Oregon, attempted to commit suicide by jumping through a closed second-story window. The fall wasn't steep enough, so he went back upstairs to a neighbor's second-story apartment and jumped through that closed window. Again, he failed so he went back to the neighbor's apartment and tried it a third time. He was rushed to the hospital but pronounced dead shortly after arrival.

○

A Los Angeles judge barred Betty Chapman, 41, from attending the Mar Vista Baptist Church forever because she repeatedly and deliberately sang off-key, loudly, while making faces at the pastor. The disagreement began in 1960 when the pastor refused to perform a wedding ceremony for a friend of Chapman's who the pastor said was under the age of consent to marry.

Kawasaki, Japan, police arrested Toyoko Terahashi, 26, in 1988 for having made as many as 100,000 crank telephone calls to her ex-husband at his office over a two-year period. As many as 200 calls per day may have been made. When police arrived at her home to arrest her, she was talking to her husband. Police overheard her yell into the phone (in Japanese), "You idiot!" She said her monthly phone bill sometimes approached half her monthly salary.

○

A government paymaster showed up at the camp of a band of Cambodian soldiers who had been stranded in a one-year battle and who had gone four months without being paid. But when it was revealed to the soldiers that the paymaster had brought no money, they killed him and then ate his body.

○

Light-skinned Theresa Mulqueen Skeeter sued her employer, a Norfolk, Virginia, municipal agency, for discriminating against her in 1983 because of race, claiming to have been born black and raised all her life with blacks. In 1987 she filed another such complaint against the agency, charging they discriminated against her because she is white.

○

In 1988 a man pulled a gun outside a Charles Town, West Virginia, convenience store minutes before it opened, fired a shot through the front window to gain entry, and forced the clerk (who was preparing for the day's business) to sell him a can of STP oil treatment.

THE ENTIRE-PRENEURIAL SPIRIT

A company whose name translates to "Transport Service for Troubled People" in Osaka, Japan, specializes in after-dark moves for wives who want to leave their husbands without alerting the neighbors and before their husbands come home from late-night dinners.

○

Among the new Japanese technology in toilets is the $2,700 paper-free Washlet Queen that cleans the user by spraying water, then blow-drying, then spraying a scent. The Asa Ichiban model toilet also analyzes urine and measures body temperature, blood pressure, and pulse.

In Seattle, Scott Bortz invented and distributed the "soft bathtub," a vinyl-covered, inch-thick padding that fits into the tub and keeps the water hot longer while providing a softer surface for relaxation. "I always did my best thinking in the bathtub," said Bortz.

○

In India, Zahid Hussein, 23, opened a rent-a-mob service in 1984 charging $20 per day to supply a large number of mostly unemployed people who will chant slogans, wave placards, and boo or cheer on cue. They earn around 5 cents a day each. If orders call for them to break the law, they get around 15 cents a day.

○

Detroit police halted a drug dealers' giveaway program in the 1970s that was intended to help revitalize the heroin distribution business, which had been falling off because of police raids. Dealers would hand out promotional cards for the businesses, and those with green stamps entitled the bearer to a free $12.50 pack of heroin as a "freak of the week."

○

Gordon and Jasmine Geisbrecht opened a restaurant in a suburb of Winnipeg, Manitoba, in 1986, called "The Outhouse," built on the theme of toilets. Toilet bowls were placed among the tables, and a toilet seat logo appeared on the menus. Health inspectors then forced the restaurant to suspend operations because it lacked adequate rest rooms.

○

American Kitchen Products Company of Maine introduced for a short while in the late 1970s "I Hate Peas," a product composed of smashed-up peas and spinach but disguised as french fries in order to entice children to eat vegetables. The product sold well for a while, but a marketing consultant said, "It became clear that the kids thought they still tasted like peas."

○

The frozen pizza plant opened by Jenos, Inc., in Wellston, Ohio, in 1982 was welcomed by townspeople, in that it employed 1,000 people, but less than a year later, the plant had generated over 400,000 pounds of pizza sludge (flour, tomato paste, cheese, pepperoni, etc.) that could not be accommodated by the sewage system. Environmental experts said it could not be buried, either, for fear it would "move" in the ground once placed there.

○

University of Wisconsin entomology professor Gene DeFoliart announced he was developing edible snack items made of insects. He said the most flavorful is the "greater was moth" larvae, dropped into a deep-fat fryer for 45 seconds and then salted. He added that insects, unlike many popular snack items, are nutritious, high in minerals and vitamins.

○

Mackie International withdrew its Chilly Bang! Bang! Juice snack package from the market after complaints from at least two state agencies. The Santa Fe Springs, California, company had developed a pistol-shaped package that allowed children to drink the juice by holding the barrel in their mouths and squeezing a trigger.

○

The Hasbro toy company withdrew its decision to market its "Zartan the Enemy" soldier doll as a "paranoid schizophrenic" that gets violent. Several mental health organizations had complained that the marketing was in poor taste and misrepresentative of mental illnesses. A Hasbro vice-president apologized.

○

Five people were accused in 1988 of trafficking in corneas supplied from at least forty-seven corpses, selling them to customers as far away as Saudi Arabia. Doctors supplying the corneas assumed they were going to a Florida tissue bank, but they were then resold for prices of up to $650 each.

○

The best-performing British exports, according to a contest in 1975, were the spaghetti the Great Yarmouth company sold to Italy and the chow mein sold by Birkenhead to Hong Kong. The pre-fab huts sold to Outer Mongolia and the tom-toms sold to several African nations by smaller companies were two other leading exports.

MAKES SENSE TO ME

Annette Montoya, 11, of Belen, New Mexico, and her parents were arrested for forgery after Annette, in the company of her father, attempted to open a bank account with a $900,000 check. The girl told sheriff's deputies that she earned the money doing "some yard work." During her interrogation she crossed her heart and said, "Hope to die if I'm lying."

○

Appealing his prison-escape conviction before the Iowa Supreme Court, a convict said that he was just trying to escape the prison's "drug-filled environment."

○

A Johannesburg court fined George Reed $60 for trespassing after he was found at 1 A.M. standing in the bedroom of

Mrs. K. van Straaten. Reed said that he went into the house to look for his pet pigeon, which he thought had flown inside.

○

A 37-year-old New York boat mechanic was convicted of the 1980 murder of a Long Island man and sentenced to life in prison. The jury did not accept his explanation that he stabbed his victim seventy-two times and ran over him with a car in "self-defense."

○

Administrative law Judge Robert Kendall refused to order the all-male Bohemian Club (which counts among its members ex-presidents of the United States as well as corporate executives) to hire female employees at its exclusive retreat. Kendall found that the club did discriminate against women but that it had a "legitimate defense" in that the club members "urinate in the open without even the use of rudimentary toilet facilities" and that a woman's presence would "alter" their behavior.

○

A Mountain View, California, teenager turned her parents in for cocaine use, saying that she used it on four occasions with them and that her father showed her how to smoke crack. The father said that he wanted his daughter "to be exposed to it at home."

○

Irish palmist Patrick Cullen died at the age of 69 in 1980. Cullen spent the 1970s developing the practice of Mammarism, or "chest clairvoyance." He claimed to be able to read a female client's future by painting her breasts and pressing them against a sheet of paper to get an imprint which he could then study.

Stopped by Massachusetts State Police for driving his car at 120 mph, John Rosano II, 23, explained that he had just purchased a roast beef sandwich and that he had to get home to eat it before it got cold.

○

Police say that a burglar in Gilroy, California, entered an apartment and proceeded to make the bed, throw out the garbage, wash the dishes, stack newspapers, and put away an ironing board and dirty clothes. The only thing taken from the apartment was a set of drapes, but the burglar replaced them by hanging a new set of curtains. The victim found a five-page note saying in part, "Dear Sir, I hope you don't mind. I cleaned your house. Don't worry. I won't take anything because my father is a duke in Spain. Don't worry. I'll clean your house for as long as you live here," signed "Prince Eddie."

○

A 34-year-old ex-marine was found guilty of sexual assault for a 1977 incident in which the martial arts expert hit and kicked a 38-year-old former nun, saying that she was attempting to cure his impotence. The man claimed that he resorted to kung fu to fend off the woman's sexual advances for several hours of off-and-on fighting. He said that she would periodically calm down and then become violent again whenever he turned her down. He said that he had to "peel her off like a damn banana."

○

The New York State Health Department fined A. Barton Hepburn Hospital $4,000 in 1984 for allowing its chief medical officer, Dr. John Bongiovanni, to continue to perform operations after a 1980 auto accident left him blind. Bongiovanni performed urinary, bladder, and prostate operations with the help of nurses and other doctors who made decisions for him.

A judge in Louisville decided a jury went "a little bit far" in recommending a sentence of 5,005 years for a man it convicted of five robberies and kidnapping. Judge Edmond Karem reduced the sentence to 1,001 years.

○

Betty Boulton of Montrose, Iowa, filed a $30 lawsuit against her neighbor, E. M. Chadwick, charging that Chadwick's beagle, Murphy, ripped through a screen door and impregnated her Scottish terrier. Said Chadwick, "She came up here asking me to pay for an abortion. I told her I didn't think Murphy was the father. If he is the father, I think we should have some say on whether she should have had an abortion without consulting Murphy or myself. I'm opposed to abortion."

○

Fred Apfel, 71, of Colonie, New York, was found innocent by reason of insanity in the 1979 ax slaying of his 71-year-old wife. Apfel said he was driven to kill her because he feared that his $40,000 bank account would be wiped out by inflation and he wanted to spare her from the resulting destitution.

NO ARTIFICIAL INGREDIENTS

A jury in Nassau County, New York, awarded $425,000 to a 24-year-old bookkeeper who claimed she lost her hair from the shock of biting into a squirming beetle in her yogurt. The woman was watching television and eating raspberry yogurt when, according to her attorney, Abraham Fuchsberg, "she felt a piece of foreign matter in her mouth. She knew it was too hard to be a raspberry, and besides it was moving."

Doctors at Indiana University discovered a patient's anemia was caused by the man's having swallowed $21.32 in coins, including 80 quarters. The zinc in the quarters caused a copper deficiency that led to the anemia, which went away when the coins were removed. The patient said he had swallowed the coins to prevent a gun in his stomach from firing. The doctors found no gun.

Doctors in Hutchinson, Kansas, needed a court's permission to remove more than a hundred metal objects, including bedsprings and razor blades, from the stomach of a prison inmate. He swallowed them in an apparent suicide attempt.

○

When residents of Princeton, West Virginia, complained their water smelled and tasted foul, workers investigated and found a decomposed body in a municipal water tank.

○

Police in Boulder arrested University of Colorado student Ellen Malmquest for feeding six live puppies to her neighbor's caged mountain lion, jaguar, and bobcat. Malmquest explained she fed the pups to the cats because she hadn't anticipated her dog's delivering such a large litter and because she's "into the foodchain thing."

○

The Khartoum representative of the International Committee of the Red Cross decided not to distribute relief supplies to thousands of Sudanese who had lived for months on grass, roots, and leaves after fleeing civil war because he was afraid of starting food riots.

○

A medical student at Jerusalem's Hebrew University was suspended after he ate a human brain to win a $12 bet. In another incident, Jay Gwaltney of Zionsville, Indiana, ate an 11-foot birch tree to win a $10,000 bet.

After Naomi and Ruth Schreiner starved to death in their Columbus, Ohio, home in 1980, police found absolutely no food in the elderly sisters' house, only little rolls of newspaper on plates, as if the women had been eating newspaper in a futile attempt at survival.

○

The Eldorado Hotel in Dawson City, Yukon, was forced to stop serving its famous sour-toe cocktail after a thirsty customer swallowed the key ingredient—a pickled human toe that hotel owner Dick Stevenson had found in a jar of rum in his cabin, where it had been left 50 years earlier by a frostbitten trapper who had shot it off to prevent gangrene.

Stevenson advertised for a new toe and bought one for $100 from an Alberta woman who sold him the middle toe of her right foot, pickled in a jar of alcohol for the 19 years since it had been amputated because of a severe corn.

○

Ten people were hospitalized after they ordered a drink called a "watermelon spot" at a nightclub in Topeka. Instead of liquor, they were served some type of dishwashing liquid from a container similar to the one in which watermelon schnapps was kept that had been mistakenly placed where the liquor was stored.

○

Ten patients, ages 69 to 98, at a nursing home in Westminster, Colorado, suffered internal burns after an employee mistakenly served oven cleaner instead of syrup on their breakfast pancakes.

○

Edith Tyler sued a restaurant in Flagstaff, Arizona, for $150,000, claiming a stuffed cabbage she ordered "apparently contained

a used rubber prophylactic." And a Newport, Tennessee, jury awarded $2,500 to Carl "Jabo" Gentry, who sued the Stokely Van-Camp Corp. after he said he found a condom in a can of the company's pork and beans.

FAR-FROM-PERFECT CRIMES

A 26-year-old man was charged with robbing a tavern in New Athens, Illinois, at gunpoint. According to sheriff's lieutenant Otto Jakob, after the robbery the man apparently lost his car keys, so he stripped to his underwear and went back inside to say he, too, had been robbed. He was nabbed because he couldn't disguise his voice enough to fool the people he had just held up.

○

William Saunders took fourteen hostages at AT&T's New York City offices because he was distraught over a child-custody fight with his wife, an AT&T employee. Thirteen of them escaped when Saunders gave them—one at a time—permission to leave the room to get a drink of water and they never returned.

Five men who tried to steal nickel from an electroplating company in Vancouver, British Columbia, were interrupted by the police. Three escaped, one was captured on the roof, and the fifth hid, ignoring five open tanks of water and climbing into a sixth tank that was closed because it was filled with a solution of cyanide and sodium hydroxide. As soon as he crouched down, the sodium hydroxide severely burned his scrotum, causing him to swallow some of the solution before jumping out of the tank in front of police. The police took him to the hospital, where he was treated for massive cyanide poisoning with stomach washouts and oxygen.

○

After burglarizing a car in Gainesville, Florida, the thief called the car's owner and offered to sell back the camera and other equipment taken. The owner wasn't at his office when he called, so the thief left several messages that he had the stolen camera and he even left his phone number. The victim called back to arrange a meeting, then called police, who arrested the burglar.

○

In Brookfield, Connecticut, at three o'clock one morning a man picked up a 25-year-old hitchhiker. Once in the car, the hitchhiker punched the man in the face, grabbed his wallet, and dashed off into the darkness. Seven hours later, the victim got a phone call from the former passenger, saying he left a money pouch with $70 in it, but no identification, on the car seat and wanted to get it back in exchange for the victim's empty wallet. The victim agreed but called the police, who arrested the hitchhiker at the exchange site.

○

A man who attempted to extort $2 million claiming to have bombs hidden in airport terminals of Charleston and Columbia, South Carolina, declined to meet face-to-face with the police to get his money. Instead, he gave them the name of his bank and his account numbers so they could deposit the funds.

○

A drunken Japanese gangster, who the authorities say boarded a flight in the Philippines with a hand grenade he wanted to smuggle into Japan, apparently decided he couldn't get the grenade past Japanese customs and tired to flush it down the toilet. Doing so caused an explosion that sent the Thai International jetliner plunging 21,000 feet and severely burned the man, who was arrested after the plane made an emergency landing.

○

Richard Brown, 22, of Boston stopped a police cruiser to report a fire in a nearby variety store. The officers guessed Brown might have started the fire himself, since he was carrying four gallons of gasoline and an unused firebomb at the time.

○

William Gillen, 26, was arrested for trying to rob a bank in Glasgow. Police put him in a lineup, but no one identified him. He was booked anyway after calling out from the lineup, "Hey, don't you recognize me?"

○

After drinking $35 worth of beer, a 32-year-old man decided to break into a store in Longmont, Colorado. He was trying to pry open the front door with a crowbar when he saw people inside staring at him and realized the store was still open.

Police in Opelousas, Louisiana, who spotted Jack Pleasant, wanted on charges of burglary and attempted auto theft, gave chase, but he managed to elude them. They arrested him a few hours later, however, when he showed up at the police station to see if anyone had turned in his wallet, which he dropped while fleeing.

○

After robbing a branch of the Mercantile Bank in Kansas City, two men hopped into a stolen car. As they started their getaway, they tossed out several boards studded with nails that pointed upward to flatten the tires of any pursuing vehicles. They then drove over one of the boards and had to abandon the car before they went two blocks.

IT SEEMED LIKE A GOOD IDEA AT THE TIME

Michael Havekost, 18, a rescue squad member, and David Domanski, 25, a volunteer firefighter, were charged with tossing rocks and cinder blocks at passing cars from overpasses along Interstate 78 in New Jersey. Police said that after hitting cars, the two would rush to the aid of their victims to make heroic rescues.

Later that same year, three young men were arrested in Illinois for dropping a 15-to-30-pound chunk of concrete from an overpass that shattered a truck windshield and decapitated a passenger. According to police, the three said "they had nothing to do, so they decided to play a game and give points for hits and near-misses." At the time, police recorded more than two dozen similar rock tosses in the area south of Chicago.

While at a party, 21-year-old Jerry Apodaca, of Dallas, accidentally shot and killed his friend, Tim Rhea, 19, when they were attempting to determine if a gun could be knocked from an assailant's hand before it could be fired. Apodaca then killed himself.

○

Christopher Paulsen, 26, died when he failed to win a one-dollar bet that he could swim underwater between two pools at an outdoor fountain in Portland, Oregon. Paulsen, who reportedly had been drinking, got caught in a conduit connecting the two pools.

○

Four members of a Buffalo, New York, junior firefighters' club admitted to setting twelve fires and reporting thousands of false alarms over a three-year period because they wanted to aid firefighters who complained of boredom.

○

Californian Robert Paul Yarrington was convicted of fraud in 1983 for hiring two friends to stage a 1979 accident in which they chopped off his left foot with an ax so that he could collect $210,000 in insurance. Yarrington successfully collected disability payments and money from three insurance companies for almost three years before his ex-girlfriend told police of the scheme. According to her story, she and another of Yarrington's friends were paid $5,000 each to go to a mountain highway, ride over Yarrington's motorcycle with a truck, and then chop his foot off. Yarrington took tranquilizers before the chopping to try to lessen the pain.

○

Two Illinois skydivers, Brian Voss, 30, and Alfred McInturff,

50, were tossing a pumpkin back and forth on their 1987 Halloween skydive when they accidently dropped it from 2,200 feet. It crashed through the roof of Becky Farrar's home, leaving orange goo all over her kitchen walls and breaking the kitchen table. Said Farrar, "If this had happened an hour earlier, we would have been sitting at the table having lunch."

○

Three Brazilian doctors were indicted for releasing radioactive material in 1987 after a scrap-metal dealer took a 500-pound lead casing filled with cesium 137, a radioactive isotope, from the rubble of their demolished clinic. When the dealer, Devair Fereira, took the casing home and dismantled it, many of his neighbors were taken with the phosphorescent glow of the cesium. Some carried it around in their pockets and showed it to friends while children rubbed it on themselves and at least one ate some of it. In all, forty people were contaminated, ten of them critically.

○

After a dorm-room inspection by an environmental health hygiene officer, four University of Minnesota football players were evicted. In the room of freshman flanker Pat Tingelhoff and junior defensive tackle Mike Pihlstrom, the officer found dried blood, animal entrails, an empty beer case filled with maggots, and body parts from a beaver, squirrels, and other animals, along with ground glass, at places an inch deep, ripped mattresses, and smashed furniture. An unnamed source told the student newspaper that a deer's head filled with maggots had been taken from beneath a bed just prior to the inspection. Tingelhoff, a wildlife management major, denied that there was a deer head or entrails in his room but disclosed that he had removed the fat from a beaver skin there.

○

A court in Maine ruled that four boys should be taken from

their father's custody because their "health, welfare, and morals" were in danger. Their father, William Radlely, allegedly ordered them to run in front of cars to fake injuries so that he could collect insurance money. The state intervened after a fifth son died while crossing a street.

○

Olympic Expositions carnival workers said that they hung Charles Smith, 18, a fellow worker, by his ankles from a crane and held him chained without food or water for two days because he was lazy. "It's just an attitude adjustment," said Tony Holmes, one of the workers. "I told him, 'You're crazy. You won't go to work.' In this carnival, everybody has got to carry his own weight."

○

Shortly after Frederick Warren argued with the driver of a tractor-trailer at a Maryland truck stop, he ran after the driver's slow-moving truck as it was leaving the stop and stabbed the left rear tire with a hunting knife. When the knife punctured the tire, the blade was blown directly back at Warren and stabbed him in the throat. He staggered for about 100 feet and died. The driver, apparently oblivious to what had happened, drove away.

○

The Michigan Board of Medicine gave a two-week suspension to Dr. Leonard Wolin after he allowed his 14-year-old son to assist him with a bladder operation on a 50-year-old woman. Wolin let his son feel a catheter balloon in the woman's bladder and had him put in two stitches when he was sewing a layer of tissue.

○

Three teenage boys in New York City stole a woman's purse

and tried to make their getaway by jumping onto a five-by-four-foot slab of ice floating down the Hudson River. They were stranded on the ice until rescued by police helicopter.

○

A 19-year-old man from Wayne, Michigan, pleaded no contest to involuntary manslaughter charges stemming from the night he threw his 14-pound bowling ball out the window of his car and through the window of an oncoming car, killing a passenger. The man told police he never intended to hit the car when he threw his "old, crummy" bowling ball out the window. Police said he and others in the car had been drinking after bowling that night.

○

A cinder block tossed from a car window killed a man in Mineola, New York, in 1988. Two college students, both 20, were charged with second-degree manslaughter for allegedly throwing the cinder block that killed 22-year-old Umansor Benitez as he stepped off a train. Investigators said that the two students were trying a stunt called "papering," in which a bundle of newspapers is thrown at passersby from a moving car and harmlessly flies apart in the air. The students reportedly used the cinder block when they couldn't find a bundle of newspapers.

○

According to the *Journal of the American Medical Association,* the deaths of two women in Seattle were attributed to the use of frequent coffee enemas. One of the women received four coffee enemas per day for fourteen days at a Mexican clinic where she was being treated following a radical mastectomy. The other woman had refused treatment for gallstones, opting instead for coffee enemas. She reportedly administered ten or twelve enemas the first night, then as many as one per hour for a few days until she suffered seizures and went into a coma. The medical examiner noted that not enough caffeine was found in the bodies to cause death but said that the "lethal effect to a large extent was due to the vast volumes of enemas given rather than the coffee per se."

○

Harold Womack, 51, of Phoenix, thought he could get his Porsche 924 out of a cinder pit at the Sunset Crater National Monument by using a 20-ton steamroller he spotted nearby. Womack drove the steamroller over to his car and hopped off to attach a chain. The steamroller kept rolling and flattened the car.

○

The foreman of a Maryland county road crew, John Richard Herzog, received a suspended sentence for hanging co-worker B. Harrison Hensley as a prank. Hensley, who blacked out during the hanging, spent weeks in therapy because of fear and anxiety stemming from the incident. At a hearing before a county board, one crew member testified that during his nineteen-year tenure he had been dumped onto the street from a salt truck, had been sprayed with burning ether, and had had his arm pushed through a glass door but that he considered the incidents horseplay and reported none of them.

○

A 15-year-old Pittsburgh boy ran away from home after receiving a bad report card, taking $74,000 in cash from his parents before he left. He was found in West Ocean City, Maryland, after a four-day spending spree, with about $53,000 left. During his stay in Ocean City he threw a party and took new friends on a limousine tour of stores, where the group purchased jewelry. Police said that "everywhere they went, they tipped, they tipped well." The boy's father was described as a "legitimate businessman" who kept large sums of cash at home.

THE GREAT PRETENDERS

An 18-year-old Peoria, Illinois, busboy was accused of impersonating a physician at two city hospitals for several months before he was found out. He allegedly examined patients, studied medical charts, and associated with nurses and other doctors at the hospitals. He also once gave a tour of one hospital to a visiting doctor and introduced him to other doctors and patients.

○

A phone caller using the names of several real doctors in Miami and who somehow had access to confidential medical records contacted as many as 200 female patients recuperating from surgery at eleven hospitals. Nicknamed "Dr. Upchuck" by police, the man instructed the women to drink two glasses of water, stick their fingers down their throats, and vomit.

○

A California man calling himself "Dr. Franklin" telephoned women in the San Francisco area saying that he had examined their blood tests and that they had a fatal disease. He then claimed to possess a drug in his blood which could cure them and said that it could be transmitted to them through sexual intercourse. At least three women fell for the story.

○

A man posing as a psychiatrist telephoned married women on Long Island, told them that their husbands were on the brink of suicide because of "deep-seated sexual problems relating to sexual fantasies," and instructed them to have sex with strangers in order to save their husbands' lives. Specifically, the caller told each woman to find a man "under 30" on the street outside her home and to invite him inside. He then gave each woman some time to do this, saying that he'd call back later. Nassau County police detective Diane Berni said that in at least three cases, the women "had some difficulty in getting a man to come into their houses, but once they accomplished this, the men were very willing to go along with the sex." The "psychiatrist" then made a second call, talked to the men, and explained the situation. He also "specified that the sex had to be carried out in the same room where the phone was because he had to instruct them in what was necessary," Berni said. He also instructed the wives not to tell their husbands about the episodes because it could be "psychologically damaging." Police said there was no evidence linking the three men to the caller.

○

Robert Hunt, 27, claimed to be Marine Capt. Robert J. Hunt, a former fighter pilot and space-shuttle astronaut. As part of his ruse, he burned some kitchen tiles and told his wife and others that they had come from the Challenger explosion. He was eventually arrested for credit-card fraud and larceny in 1989 but not before using his fake identity to carry him through several speaking engagements and marriages. Hunt once met with the lord mayor of Dublin, where he was made an honorary citizen.

Santa Clara County, California, investigators charged the adopted son of 84-year-old Myrtle Reid, a woman with cardiovascular disease, with her murder. He allegedly impersonated a heart surgeon who advised Reid to stop taking her medication and to jump up and down for 15 minutes to relieve stomach pain. The adopted son stood to inherit her $350,000 estate.

○

Murder suspect Dennis J. Hannuksela, 29, escaped from police custody in Duluth, Minnesota, when, being taken for a hospital visit, he dropped his crutches and took off "like a jack rabbit." Said Sgt. Tom Person, the county jail supervisor, "The deputy didn't have him in handcuffs because you don't handcuff a man on crutches."

○

Police suspected that 47-year-old John Irish was the man who posed as a Roman Catholic priest, "Father John Irish," at the scene of several air disasters in 1987 to steer families of victims to use the services of a certain Florida lawyer. Northwest Airlines claimed that the man defrauded the airline of $1,100 in hotel and food charges. The "priest" was also reportedly seen talking to car accident victims.

○

On the second day of his trial for arson and assault, defendant Tyrone Robinson smeared his face with used toilet paper and ran at the jury, causing the judge to declare a mistrial. Robinson then spent over six months rocking, moaning, shuddering, and speaking in an unintelligible language in an attempt to convince a court that he was mentally ill. The day before his new trial was to begin, Robinson, a man who supposedly no longer knew how to talk, requested a plea-bargain meeting with the Assistant United States Attorney, Michael Brittin. "I thought I could beat this thing," he told Brittin, "but it's clear to me that you're not going to let go."

○

Baltimore Judge Hilary Caplan voided the marriage of Liberian Prince M. K. Ofosu-Appiah, 28, to Delores Buchanan, on the grounds that Buchanan was a man. The prince, who claimed that he never saw Buchanan nude and never consummated the marriage, discovered that Delores was a man when he saw that her birth certificate had "male" in the section identifying sex.

○

A 17-year-old Memphis woman was married for four months before discovering that her husband was a 19-year-old woman. According to a clergyman involved in the case, the woman said that her husband never let her see "him" naked because he was supposedly deformed by a football injury. The bride reportedly became suspicious when some of her husband's friends referred to him as "Harriet."

○

In 1989 jazz musician Billy Tipton died of a bleeding ulcer, leaving an ex-wife and three adopted sons. While the funeral director was preparing the body for burial, he discovered the 74-year-old saxophonist-pianist was really a woman. "He'll always be Dad," said one of Tipton's boys.

THE SPORTS SECTION

Pro golfer Homero Blancas once hit a ball out of the rough in a tournament and saw it hit a palm tree and then lodge in the brassiere of a female spectator. (Blancas asked fellow golfer Chi Chi Rodriguez what he should do, whereupon Rodriguez reportedly replied, "I think you should play it.")

○

An April 1967 spring training game between the Chicago Cubs and the California Angels in Las Vegas was called off in the ninth inning (with the score tied, 10–10) on account of sunshine. (Pitchers complained they couldn't read the catcher's signs because of the glare.)

○

Oakland Athletics' pitcher Dave Stewart, when he was a member of the Texas Rangers team, was arrested in Los Angeles for lewd conduct with another man. According to police, Stewart was receiving oral sex from a man Stewart mistakenly believed was a woman because of the dress and wig he was wearing.

○

A libel lawsuit by former major-league pitcher Art Ditmar was dismissed by a state supreme court. Ditmar had been identified in a famous beer commercial, per the radio play-by-play background, as the pitcher who gave up the World Series–ending home run by Bill Mazeroski in 1960, when the pitcher actually was Ralph Terry. The mistake was made by the 1960 announcer and perpetuated by the beer company.

○

Army defeated the University of Pennsylvania in a 1983 college swim meet that was conducted entirely by telephone because of near blizzard conditions. Since travel was virtually impossible, each team swam heats, and the times were compared.

○

In Goodwater, Alabama, home of three casket manufacturers, casket races were held in 1983 and 1988. The object of the races was that a "live corpse" in each of the caskets had to maneuver through an obstacle course while holding a glass of water, being careful not to spill over one ounce during the race.

○

Minor-league catcher Dave Bresnahan had his baseball career end in 1987 over a prank while he was with the Williamsport, Pennsylvania, team of the Eastern League. With a runner on third base, Bresnahan reached in his pocket for a potato he had hidden there and fired it over third base, enticing the runner to run home, whereupon Bresnahan pulled out the real baseball and tagged him out. When the umpire realized what had happened, he ruled the runner safe, and the next day Bresnahan was fined $50 for bringing disrespect to the game and also was given his unconditional release. (Bresnahan was batting only .184 at the time.)

○

At least one child was killed during a 1989 fad that swept Tel Aviv and Jerusalem in which bands of boys would dash in front of speeding cars to see who could be the most daring. Several versions of the game were played: In one, the boys lay down, and the last one to get up when a car came along won. In the most popular version, a candy bar was placed in the street, and the boy who came closest to getting hit got to eat the candy bar.

○

In Brazil over 200 deaths during 1987–88, and over 500 injuries, were attributed to "train surfing," in which young boys would run nimbly atop mass-transit trains in Rio de Janeiro. Some of the deaths involved falls from the trains, but others occurred when the trains passed over high-voltage electric wires. One youth interviewed by the *Wall Street Journal* admitted the game was dangerous but said, "I got used to it, and I can't stop." The trains' top speed is 75 mph.

○

After a 1988 game, the wives of Seattle Supersonics basketball players Alton Lister and Dale Ellis exchanged punches while comparing their respective husbands' salaries. Just a few days earlier, the wife of Los Angeles Laker Byron Scott fought with wives of several members of the Los Angeles Clippers after her husband's team had just lost a close game.

FIRE

Three people in Fordyce, Arkansas, were injured when three toilets in separate buildings exploded after an accidental hookup allowed propane gas to enter the water system. Flushing released bubbles of the highly flammable gas, which ignited from some source of open flame near the toilets. "Things come and things go," Fire Chief Roy Wayne Moseley said, "but when a man sees water burning, maybe it's time to go."

There was no fire, but people using the rest rooms at the King County, Washington, courthouse were pretty hot when two dozen toilets and urinals erupted after they were flushed because an air compressor was mistakenly connected to a water line.

○

Eight years after being convicted of arson, 31-year-old David DiIorio was appointed to the North Providence, Rhode Island, fire department. A police check had failed to turn up any criminal record because DiIorio's name was misspelled.

○

A Detroit man sued the city fire department for letting his apartment burn down while two firefighters who were supposed to be fighting the fire were fighting each other. Alan Ruprecht said the first firefighter entered his burning apartment carrying a hose, but when he opened the nozzle no water came out. The first firefighter got mad at a second firefighter for not turning on the water and began beating him over the head with his helmet. Meanwhile, the blaze destroyed the apartment.

○

Truck driver James R. Shaw was on Interstate 5 near Medford, Oregon, when his brakes caught fire. He pulled into a rest area and tried to douse the flames with his fire extinguisher but was unsuccessful. He hopped back into the blazing truck and raced down the road, hoping the wind would blow out the fire, but was forced to stop after nine miles when the flames completely engulfed his truck. The burning truck blocked the highway for three hours.

○

An investigator from the state fire marshal's office discovered 256 fire-safety problems, including a lack of smoke detectors and fire alarms, at seven fire stations in Manchester, New Hampshire, during a 1989 inspection. The inspector even cited the city's fire-prevention office for hazardous extension cords. The year before, one of the fire department's oldest stations burned down while its crew was on a call.

○

Gary Douglas Stranz admitted setting the fire that destroyed the Round Lake Presbyterian Church. He explained that he ran into the church to avoid a man who was making homosexual advances toward him and started the fire to draw attention to his predicament.

Rags soaked in linseed oil ignited spontaneously at a restaurant in Alameda, California, after hours. Before firefighters arrived, heat from the fire popped the tops on bottles of ten cases of beer, sending out a stream of suds that doused the flames. A similar case occurred in Miramar, Florida, when a fire started at a day-care center after a table fan short-circuited. Before firefighters arrived, heat from the fire ruptured a fire extinguisher hanging above the fan, spraying its chemical contents all over the smoke-filled room and putting out the blaze.

○

Despondent over an argument with his girlfriend, Anthony Dyke committed suicide by dousing himself with gasoline in the living room of his family's New York City home and setting himself on fire. His mother and stepbrother also died, another stepbrother suffered second-degree burns, and five other relatives were injured in the blaze, which spread to the rest of the house, according to fire department official John Mulligan, when Dyke ran upstairs "in a ball of fire, possibly to get into the shower, maybe to extinguish the flame."

○

A Salt Lake City jury convicted Debbie Bergwerff of aggravated arson despite defense attorney Robert VanSciver's contention that the blaze, which caused $55,000 damage to her home, started when bird droppings from her two parakeets, mixed with spilled lamp oil, spontaneously burst into flames inside a faulty vacuum cleaner.

○

When firefighters in Hallandale, Florida, raced off on an emergency call, they forgot to turn off a burner on the firehouse stove that was heating oil for frying potatoes. The result was a blaze that caused $10,000 worth of damage.

"We tell people not to do that kind of stuff," Acting Battalion Chief Martin McMahon said. "We all come from the human race. We make mistakes."

○

A woman in Bloomington, Illinois, called police to report that her shoes were on fire. After the responding officer beat out the blaze with a stick, the woman explained she had wanted a hot barbecue sandwich and decided to use her shoes to heat it. She was charged with unlawful burning within city limits.

SURGES OF TESTOSTERONE

A Hicksville, New York, school-bus driver was accused in 1989 of molesting several child passengers over a period of time by establishing a "kiss the driver" day.

○

A man was charged in New Orleans in 1982 with a scheme in which he fondled the breasts of women who indicated interest in working as instructors on a project he had. He had posed as a doctor working to help the elderly learn to burp properly, and younger females were preferred as instructors, but first he had to be sure they could burp properly themselves.

○

In an attempt to encourage their two female gorillas to breast-feed their babies, officials of the Columbus, Ohio, Zoo had a woman stand in front of the glass-walled gorilla house and breastfeed her own child so the gorillas could see. But the zoo's male gorilla, Oscar, was the most entranced by the woman and had to be enticed away from the viewing area by an extra allotment of bananas.

○

A 1986 medical journal article described the case of a man who reported to a hospital in Italy with a strand of spaghetti in his urethra. He had reported a burning sensation and "abnormal curvature of the penis during erection."

○

An electronics engineer was arrested in San José after having tunneled through attics in a row of condominiums where he lived and drilled tiny holes in the bedroom ceilings of several units. One couple heard what they described as a mouse and opened the crawlspace in the attic to discover the man, who got away but was apprehended shortly afterward.

○

In 1989 Salt Lake City police apprehended a 22-year-old man at the Tracy Aviary and charged him with sexually assaulting and then killing an exotic demoiselle crane.

○

The lawyer of former Chelsea, England, mayor John Brooks said Brooks was to be excused for his fondness for slapping women's bottoms. "Every healthy normal vigorous male is a bottom slapper in mind if not in deed," said Roger Gray. Brooks was turned in in 1974 by 19-year-old Sue Carr, who responded to an ad for crewmates on Brooks's cruiser and was offered an additional $24 if she would allow him to spank her.

Arthur Sharland, 77, was found dead in West London, sitting in an armchair with two wires from an electric socket attached to his nipples with crocodile clips. A mass of tiny scars, some quite old, suggested that he had indulged in the habit for many years and might simply have misestimated the voltage.

○

A report in a 1987 medical journal describes the case of surgery performed on a 20-year-old man who walked into an emergency room after his lover had given him an enema containing concrete mix. The surgeons marveled after removing the concrete cast of the inside of the rectum—perfect, they wrote, except for a chipping at one end, which, when further probed, revealed a white plastic Ping-Pong ball, which they speculated was used to "retain the enema."

○

In 1989 the Florida Department of Conservation considered withdrawing approval for commercial "swim and hug" programs that entrepreneurs were running in the Florida Keys in which humans could cavort with dolphins. That is because of increased complaints that male dolphins were becoming sexually aroused while alongside female customers. A Miami secretary reported that one male dolphin had rubbed up against her amorously. "He liked me *a lot*," she said.

A POOR CHOICE OF WORDS

Commenting on proposed legislation to require drivers to notify the owners of domestic animals that they injure or kill, Iowa state senator James Gallagher said he could understand stopping for dogs but not for cats. "You squish a cat and you go on," Gallagher said. "I think we're overcomplicating life."

○

A 15-year-old boy in Richmond, Texas, was certified to stand trial as an adult in the beating death of his 39-year-old mother, who had been struck a dozen times with a baseball bat. Asked at the hearing why he was in custody, the teenager reportedly responded, "I played a little baseball with my mother."

William Lantz, 37, of Rochester, New York, was shot and killed with an arrow shot by his neighbor, Steven Merkel. A witness said that both men had been drinking beer on her porch when Merkel went to his house and came outside with a bow and arrow. When Merkel "kept saying he wanted to shoot somebody," Lantz said, "Go ahead, Rambo, I don't think you have the guts to do it."

○

After being injured by the same pet buffalo that mauled his son a year earlier, Gerald Assel of Bismarck, North Dakota, said that the animal would have to be destroyed. "He was a pet, but he turned against us," said Assel. "You can never trust a buffalo."

○

After his arraignment for the flashlight beating death of his dwarf wife in 1981, convicted murderer Billy Jack Shelby, 44, of Nashville, a double-amputee, said, "I didn't kill nobody this time. I'm looking for a little justice and looking for some legs." After his conviction for the murder, Shelby, being led from the courtroom, shouted to the judge, "I'll see you in hell."

○

While awaiting Congressional confirmation of his appointment to head the Office of Juvenile Justice and Delinquency Prevention in the first Reagan administration, Alfred Regnery defended a bumper sticker on his car as just a joke. The sticker read, "Have You Slugged Your Kid Today?"

Commenting on the scene of a truck accident in which 44,000 pounds of pig carcasses were dumped over the highway near San Bernardino, California Highway Patrol officer John Savage said, "These little piggies didn't make it to market."

Recalling the accident in which he ran over his 18-month-old son Dewey with a 3-ton bulldozer, Melvin McCall, 34, of Green Cove Springs, Florida, said "His little eyes bulged out. . . . He looked so flat. He just looked like he was spread out all over the ground." The nearby hospital termed Dewey's survival and recovery a "freak occurrence."

○

In an effort to evade health department investigators, British artist Robert Lenkiewicz hid the embalmed body of his 72-year-old friend Edward McKenzie. "When the legal questions have been sorted out, I will bring him home, where he will remain for the rest of my life, something like a large paperweight in the library," Lenkiewicz said.

○

Convicted murderer James Hamblen, sitting on Florida's death row, said, "I can hardly wait to sit in Old Sparky [the nickname of the state's electric chair]. I'm curious about it. I think it's spiffy."

○

A former nurse's aide from Tyler, Texas, was accused of murdering five nursing-home patients at a facility near Grand Rapids, Michigan, for the "emotional release" it gave her. According to a co-worker who acted as a lookout during the murders, the nurse's aide killed the patients "to relieve [her] stress if she was having a bad day."

○

Ohio veterinarian Marshall Pettibone, who uses a freeze-drying machine to preserve dead pets, said, "There's no sense in getting a new cat every ten years or so when you can have the same one for fifty or sixty years!" Said Oramae Lewis, who had her cat Felix freeze-dried after he was run over by an eighteen-wheel tractor-trailer, "He's just like he was in real life except he's a little flatter in the middle."

○

Leonard DiCicco, 23, described his associate, Kevin Mitnick, 25, a computer hacker accused of infiltrating computer systems in the United States and England, as "a big fat slob of a guy who couldn't get through a day without breaking into a computer somewhere. All he did was eat Fat Burgers, drink Slurpees, and work on computers."

○

Gerald Chapple, 34, was charged with attacking Bill Gibson, his sister's 38-year-old boyfriend and Christmas dinner host, in 1987, biting off half of his left ear. The incident followed a Christmas day drinking session. Asked by his sister what happened, Chapple said, "I ate it, yum, yum." Chapple reportedly told police, "I ate his ear—his nose was next."

○

In 1978 a Republican candidate for county sheriff in Washington state, Joe Taylor, collapsed at a candidates' forum after criticizing his opponent, Detective John Kozar. Both Kozar and Sheriff Bill Williams then administered heart massage and mouth-to-mouth resuscitation in a failed attempt to save Taylor. "Death is death," said Williams. "It transcends politics."

FIRST THINGS FIRST

Officials of Nigeria Airways, trying to freshen its image and increase travelers' confidence, decided the first step should be to change the airline's symbol from an elephant to an eagle.

○

The woman whom Catholic priest Gene Jakubek confessed to having had sex with four times in two years insisted they actually had sex twice a month for four years. In fairness to Jakubek, she added that he did give up sex for Lent.

○

In Scranton, Pennsylvania, Sandra Kaushas stabbed her husband Edward five times after he refused to go out for pizza during the first half of a 1985 Miami–New England football playoff game. He told police he had offered to get chicken at halftime, but that didn't satisfy her.

○

A week before Super Bowl XXIII, longtime San Francisco 49ers fan Les Boatwright died of a heart attack, holding two tickets to the game. Knowing Boatwright wouldn't have wanted to miss the game, his two sons took the tickets and brought his ashes to Miami's Joe Robbie Stadium in an urn.

○

In Houston, 37-year-old Delores Douglas was watching a Disney movie on television when her fiancé, Eddie Harris, switched the channel to watch Super Bowl XXIV. Douglas became so

upset that she stabbed him in the neck with a barbecue fork. That same day in Jonesboro, Georgia, Mary Helen Holloway shot herself in the head following an argument with her husband, Gary. Rather than report her death right away, he waited until after he had watched San Francisco's 45-point rout of Denver at his mother-in-law's home, then called police the next morning. "I can't explain this wild story," said medical examiner investigator Jim Mabe. "That game was so boring."

○

According to the official New China News, Mao Tse-tung's wife, Chiang Ching, was playing poker in Shensi province in 1976 when she received a telephone call that her husband was near death and that transportation was arranged for her to fly the 200 miles to Peking to be at his bedside. The news agency reported that she returned to her game and continued playing as though nothing had happened until others finally convinced her to leave.

○

All Nelson McIntosh packed for a 90-minute boat ride from one island in the Bahamas to another was two beers, and they were gone when a storm disabled his boat and left him adrift in the Atlantic for seven weeks. When fishermen found McIntosh, who had gone from 180 pounds to only 80 pounds and was malnourished, dehydrated, and suffering from hypothermia, the first thing the 27-year-old lobsterman asked for was another beer. "I am a beer drinker," he explained.

○

Two suspected Red Brigade terrorists, kept caged during their trial in Turin, Italy, as a security measure, nevertheless managed to have sex while court was in session. Angela Vai and

Raffaele Fiore reportedly engaged in a sexual act in the cage while sixteen other defendants gathered in front of the bars to hide the couple.

○

A 57-year-old pilot and his female passenger died when their Cessna 172 slammed into a cliff along the shore of Lake Mead, near Las Vegas. Authorities investigating the crash, which occurred shortly past midnight on a clear night with a nearly full moon, concluded from the position of the bodies in the wreckage and certain injuries to the pilot that the passenger was performing an act of oral sex at the moment of impact.

○

A charter pilot in line waiting to take off from Manchester, England, reportedly suffered a heart attack but continued on with the flight to Spain rather than lose his takeoff slot. According to the Royal Air Force Institute of Medicine, the unidentified pilot said afterward he had felt an intense chest pain and asked his co-pilot to take over the flight to Malaga and to keep an eye on him.

○

In Paris, when the pilot of a French jetliner bound for Marseilles announced to the 280 passengers as the plane was ready for takeoff that he had decided to join a strike by his company's ground crew, the passengers seized the aircraft and announced they were holding the pilot hostage until either he took off or the airline found them another flight.

○

Police ordered the martial arts movie *A Force of One* stopped at a Miami theater after one member of the audience stabbed another to death for stepping on his toe. They wanted to search for clues, but the other patrons began stomping their feet impatiently in protest. "People who had paid became very upset and started yelling when we turned the lights up," Detective Richard Bohan said. "They just didn't care. They were more concerned with seeing the movie."

○

An ice-cream vendor in Chicago who was robbed of $75 when two armed men jumped aboard his truck and shot him twice said he also lost $195 worth of ice cream when about a hundred neighborhood children helped themselves, ignoring his pleas for help. "I yelled at them to stop, but it didn't do any good," said Ebenezer Obomanu. "It took about 15 or 20 minutes for them to empty my truck. It was a great celebration."

In Los Angeles, several youths beat ice cream vendor Victorino A. Parades, 55, to death. Witnesses said that as soon as Parades's body fell unconscious and the gang fled, two dozen or so onlookers rushed the van and stole ice cream, candy, and cash.

In East San José, California, 65-year-old Raymond Nott, who ran a candy store in his home, died of a heart attack. He lived alone, so the coroner removed the body and sealed off the house. Three days later, police said, fifty or sixty area youngsters broke the glass sliding door at the rear of Nott's town house, then used a long piece of pipe with a hook on it to reach through the door's sturdy grid of security bars and pull boxes of candy from shelves and counters in the kitchen to where they could remove them. Police officer Don Harris, summoned to the scene by neighbors, said he found "candy strewn all over the floor. It was too much temptation for little kids who love candy."

THE WORLD AS I SEE IT

Chicago missionary Michele Schwartz, 41, was acquitted of murder in the shooting of her husband, the Reverend Charles Jones. The killing happened during an argument over housework and the question of who had saved more souls. When police arrived at the scene, they found Jones dead and Schwartz reading the Bible. At her trial Schwartz said that Jones had beaten her and at one point was "stamping on [her] liver."

○

Phil Phillips, author of *Turmoil of the Toybox*, believes that Satan is trying to gain control of children's minds through their toys. Phillips says that Yoda from "Star Wars" encourages what he sees as the "occult" beliefs of Zen Buddhism, Taoism, Islam, and Judaism. He also thinks that the unicorns of *My Little Pony* are symbolic of the Antichrist and that Care-Bears promote Eastern religious concepts, and he notes that Papa Smurf uses spells and incantations. To Phillips, Masters of the Universe and He-Man usurp God's role as the universe's actual master.

A De Kalb County, Georgia, Superior Court ruled that Gary Eugene Duda, 35, could change his first name to "Zippidy." Duda said that he had already been called "Zippidy" by friends for most of his life.

○

St. Louis police arrested a 38-year-old man for allegedly hitting Sharon Copeland, 35, with a hammer while she was sunbathing in her back yard. According to police, the man told her, "I don't like sunbathers." He told police, "The metric system angers me."

○

Following the shooting deaths of a rural Wisconsin family, police searched for a missing 70-year-old relative who reportedly purchased .22-caliber ammunition a few weeks prior to the incident while remarking that the family watched too many pornographic videos.

○

On August 19, 1987, 34-year-old Gary Stollman of Tallahassee, Florida, walked onto a live news broadcast on KNBC-TV in Los Angeles, pointed a toy pistol at newsman David Horowitz, and forced him to read a statement. While the station blacked out the rest of its broadcast, Horowitz read the statement, which warned that the CIA and "alien forces" from outer space were plotting against the government of the United States and "possibly the human race itself."

○

The Citizens Committee for the Right to Keep and Bear Arms petitioned the Vatican in 1987 to name St. Gabriel Possenti as the "patron of handgunners." St. Gabriel reportedly used a show of marksmanship in 1859 to disarm a group of soldiers in Italy.

○

The Schiller Institute, in an attempt to "defeat the growing scourge of Satanism internationally," supports "the international campaign to lower tuning pitch to A = 432," as was preferred by Giuseppe Verdi. The current standard in the United States is A = 440, in Europe, A = 442. Paul Schmitz of the institute says that the human singing voice is supposed to be pitched at instrumental A = 432 but that record company executives, the people who produce "heavy metal satanic rock," have raised the pitch.

○

Adelaide Sanford, a black woman who is a member of New York State's education policy-setting board, believes that "the melanin in the skin of children of African ancestry bonds with narcotics and causes the addiction." She later said that she did not mean that blacks are more addiction-prone than whites but merely thinks that the possibility of such a chemical link should be researched.

○

In revenge for England's closing of the Libyan embassy in London, Col. Muammar el-Qaddafi ordered that England be deleted from all Libyan maps in the mid-1980s. In its place was put a new arm of the North Sea, bordered by Scotland and Wales.

○

While president of the Philippines, Ferdinand Marcos spent years moving around provincial and municipal boundaries in an attempt to draw his image into the map of the northern Philippines. One map published by the *Daily Globe* showed the profile of Marcos facing west toward his home province of Ilocos Norte.

○

Daniel Pucheta, a sorcerer, explained why he failed to summon Satan to a witchcraft convention in Mexico in 1981: "We should have started at midnight, not 1:30 in the morning. The devil does not keep Mexican time."

○

Jurgen Hergert, 44, known as the "King of Snakes," broke his old record when he sat in a glass cage of snakes for 100 days. Inside the cage were twenty-four rattlesnakes, vipers, puff adders, and cobras. During his stay, one Indian cobra killed three other snakes. While in the cage, he lost nine pounds and averaged only two or three hours of sleep per night, and his girlfriend called off their engagement.

MEDICAL MILESTONES

James Sexton was released from a Santa Rosa, California, hospital in 1987 in good health shortly after being shot six times in the head by his former roommate, Daniel Frost. The six .22-caliber bullets were still in his head, but none penetrated the brain, and none required removal.

In tumor news:

- Luis Enrique Soltero, 19, of Tijuana, Mexico, had a tumor the size of a peach removed from the middle of his head in a San Diego hospital and was so impressed afterward that he wanted to go to medical school.

- A 380-pound woman had a 200-pound cyst, 36 inches in diameter, removed from her abdomen in San Francisco. It had been growing for fifteen years, since she was 15.

- Physicians operating on an elderly woman for what they thought was a malignant ovarian cyst found instead a cyst surrounding a diamond that measured ⅛ inch across.

Doctors guessed it was dropped into her reproductive tract when she had a baby by cesarean section fifty years before.

- A Lewistown, Pennsylvania, woman who weighed nearly 600 pounds and who had to be taken to the hospital by fire and rescue workers had a 280-pound cyst removed. When called to the home, one rescue worker thought "there were two people lying in bed." Workers had to knock down a wall to extricate her from the house.

○

In 1979, surgeons in Tampa removed the entire cranium of a 6-year-old girl whose head had swollen to the size of a 35-pound watermelon. They reconstructed it to a smaller size before reattaching it. In 1983 a "naturopath" in Alberta, Canada, inserted a balloon up the nose of a 20-month-old girl to increase the size of her skull, which the man said was abnormally small. When she died, he was sentenced to a day in jail and a $1,000 fine.

○

A Navy hospital corpsman was convicted of assault and punished for sewing a sailor's ear to his pillow in a Virginia Beach, Virginia, clinic. Supposedly, the prank was in punishment for his violent behavior earlier at the clinic.

○

Dr. James C. Burt retired after investigations by the Ohio State Medical Board of his use of "vaginal reconstruction surgery" on numerous patients without their consent. According to Burt's 1975 book *The Surgery of Love*, a woman would become "horny like [a mouse]" if her clitoris were moved closer to the vaginal opening.

Lynn Ray Collins, mute for seventeen years after being hit by a car, regained his speech after falling against a glass door in Albertville, Alabama, in 1989. He was moved to speak to paramedics as he watched three pints of blood gushing from his head wound.

O

Doctors worked more than seven hours to close farmworker Chris Haines's mouth in Little Thurlow, England, after he had yawned too widely and couldn't get it closed. Haines could only make gurgling noises during the procedure and thus could not communicate with doctors.

O

A Petersburg, Virginia, dentist lost his license to practice in 1989 after complaints that he had left broken anesthesia needles inside patients' mouths and that once he had administered anesthesia to a root-canal patient and then gone to sleep in another room so soundly that the patient had trouble waking him when he went looking for him.

O

Forthman Murff, 74, managed to survive an accident in which his head was nearly severed, dangling by his carotid arteries and the cervical spine, in Tupelo, Mississippi. He had fallen onto a chain saw but managed to throw off the saw, get up, drive to a hospital (despite a broken leg), and be treated within an hour of the accident. His windpipe and esophagus were cut clean through.

O

Arthur "Ben" Gross, 70, was cut nearly in half by a circular saw accident near St. Louis but was eating again only six days later. The incision started at the left rib cage and cut through his liver, bowel, colon, scrotum, and rectum.

○

An Australian medical journal reported on items that had been removed from rectums of men at local hospitals and gave some men's explanations. A man with a jar of petroleum jelly in his rectum said he inserted it to remove itchiness. A 63-year-old man said he had slipped in the shower and landed on a lemon. A 45-year-old man said he also had slipped in the shower and landed on a plastic bicycle handle grip.

○

A Virginia medical journal reported that during a routine rectal procedure in 1978 in which polyps on the colon are cut with heat drawn from a device inserted into the rectum, a 68-year-old patient released enough gas to cause a small explosion inside the colon—propelling the patient forward several feet and sending the doctor and his assistant several feet backward into a wall.

VISIONS OF MARY AND JESUS

In 1983 Josephine Taylor of Constance Lake, Ontario, said that she saw the image of Jesus Christ on her bathroom floor. Taylor says that one morning she looked down and saw the image, formed by dark spots on the cement floor. Edgar Sutherland, an associate of the village minister, said that the image was only worn linoleum adhesive. About 3,000 Canadians came to see for themselves.

Thousands of people flocked to Arlene Gardner's trailer in Estill Springs, Tennessee, in 1987 to see the image of Christ on Arlene's General Electric freezer, which was on the front deck of the house. Each day after dusk, a neighbor's porch light apparently caused a bearded face to appear on the side of the freezer. Gardner claimed to have had a dream in which

Christ told her that "he connected that porch light to my freezer and turned my freezer into a TV by electricity. He made it a TV. That's how I knew he wanted this vision on television for the world to see." The family refused offers to charge viewers.

◯

The image of the Blessed Virgin Mary reportedly appeared on the front wall of the home of Alvaro and Petra Zamora in Bakersfield, California, drawing hundreds of people a night. The Fresno Catholic Diocese took no position on the faint white image, with Monsignor J. Wayne Hayes saying, "We don't know what it is."

◯

Beginning on Christmas Eve 1988 and lasting well into the new year, a nocturnal light in a firewood yard in Harris County, Texas, was the source for many sightings for Jesus and/or Mary. More than 1,000 spectators showed up for the first two weeks to view the light, located between logs and stacks of firewood. They watched a light radiating a blue, beige, and white diamond image in which some saw Jesus with a crown of thorns and some-times accompanied by Mary. The light apparently was reflected off a discarded tabletop near the back of the lot. But the tabletop faced south and apparently projected the image to the west. The family donated money left at the image to the homeless.

Also in December 1988, John and Mary New of Sulphur, Louisiana, reported the vision of a pregnant Mary on the trunk of their magnolia tree. The image reportedly appeared when a streetlight shone through the leaves of the tree. From 300 to 400 spectators showed up each night for a look.

◯

The Perez family of Taft, Texas, said that the image of Jesus appeared in the swirls of ceiling plaster in a room in their home. Petra Perez said that the image, of Christ's face and "sacred heart," was best seen by kneeling and looking through a window.

○

Jim Armour, administrator of the Walker County Medical Center in Jasper, Alabama, said that at least 10,000 people came to view what some believed to be the face of Jesus on the door of the center's recovery room. "The people who work here do believe the door is different than what it was. I believe it is different," said Armour. "We have a housekeeper who dusts that door and she says it wasn't like that before." The image was first seen by the praying relative of a motorcycle accident victim.

○

In 1983 some residents of the South Side of San Antonio got fed up with noisy crowds gathering nightly to view what they believed to be the image of Mary. One resident, Candelario Gutierrez, had flood lights installed and turned them on to dispel the image and disperse the spectators. Gutierrez charged that the image was merely the result of a porch light reflecting off the bumper of a '75 Chevrolet.

○

In New Mexico in 1977, a woman claimed that the image of Jesus appeared on a tortilla that had been burned in a skillet.

○

The image of Jesus was reportedly seen on the side of a Fostoria, Ohio, soybean oil tank. The image was never seen again after the tank was painted.

In 1981 the image of Christ being crucified attracted crowds to Santa Fe Springs, California. It was eventually determined that the image was caused by two streetlights shining on a bush and a real estate sign.

○

About 3,000 people gathered in a vegetable field near Tickfaw, Louisiana, on March 12, 1989, in hopes of seeing the Blessed Virgin Mary. The crowds gathered in response to visions experienced by Alfredo Raimondo, 52, a pipe fitter, who claimed that Mary appeared to him and told him to go to Tickfaw to honor St. Joseph. Many in the field that Sunday did claim to have seen something. Some, who had taken photographs of the sun, showed the results around. "See, here's the Blessed Mother," said one woman, pointing to a photo. "I think she's following the sun. And look, what do you see here? It's St. Peter. See his hat and his face?"

ON THE JOB

Officials in Jacksonville hired twenty-three people to work the weekend before Christmas 1989, doing nothing but flushing the 503 toilets at the Gator Bowl to prevent the stadium's water pipes from freezing.

○

A review of the output of the nation's first two poet laureates, Robert Penn Warren and Richard Wilbur, disclosed that despite collecting a salary of $35,000 a year, neither produced a single line of verse while poet laureate. When Warren accepted the first laureateship in 1986, he commented, "I don't expect you'll hear me writing any poems to the greater glory of Ronald and Nancy Reagan. Why should I?"

A reporter asked if he at least planned to visit schools and talk to youngsters about poetry. "Of course not!" Warren protested. "That stuff's a lot of work!"

In Dallas, a 25-year-old police officer posing as a high school student as part of an undercover drug operation was nabbed for being tardy and sent to the principal's office. Told he could choose between a paddling and detention, the officer was forced to take the spanking because detention would have interfered with a scheduled drug buy.

○

Two men had little trouble robbing an armored van in Livonia, Michigan. They simply pulled open the van's back doors, which were unlocked and held shut by rubber bands, which police said the van's security guard used to avoid going to all the trouble of unlocking and locking the doors at each stop.

○

Clark Dill, sanitation director of Fayetteville, North Carolina, came to work to find that despite his department's having been locked and deserted, switchboard computer records showed more than a hundred telephone calls had been placed overnight from two telephone extensions, most within seconds of each other. An investigation disclosed that the culprit wasn't burglars or hackers but two Coca-Cola machines.

Both had been equipped with computers to let the local distributor know when it was time for a refill. "The Coke machines were calling the computer at the Coke company, and for some reason the computer just wouldn't answer," Dill said. "So the machines just kept calling and calling."

○

Authorities in Rome arrested a 32-year-old waiter who was giving restaurant patrons menus that contained nude photographs of himself.

A New York Transit Authority supervisor who stopped working continued to collect paychecks for a year. William Uhrin, a deputy supervisor in a Queens subway yard, was transferred to a bus depot in the Bronx in 1986. He had to pick up his paycheck in Brooklyn, where the Transit Authority's bus operation is based.

Later that year, he told his superiors in the Bronx that he was being transferred back to the Queens subway yard. Since neither the Bronx nor the Queens facilities expected Uhrin, they never reported him absent, and he continued picking up his checks in Brooklyn. He was caught only when he tried to get off the payroll by resigning.

○

An even more ambitious worker was Luigi Cincotta, who held a job with the Palermo Health Council in Italy. In the ten years before he was finally fired in 1980, he managed to miss work a total of five of them, citing illness, convalescence, and deaths in the family as excuses for his absences. Actually, he was working a side job as a furniture salesman.

○

A sewage treatment plant worker in Ohio who said his job is so easy that he works just half an hour a day spent $1,311 to take out newspaper ads expressing his appreciation. "Thanks Toledo. For 18 years of generous wages, very liberal working conditions, and much more at your sewage plant," read the ads taken out by 47-year-old James Pieper.

○

George Libera, a railroad worker in Brainerd, Minnesota, said that most days he and others whose jobs were eliminated but whose employment was protected by a merger agreement sit from 7 A.M. to 3 P.M. in a room doing nothing. "It sounds like a good deal, but it's not," Libera said. "I actually leave there feeling more physically and mentally exhausted than if I'd worked eight hours."

The men aren't allowed to play cards, read, or nap, although they can talk to one another. On the plus side, Libera said that in 1984 he was being paid $100 a day and that he is guaranteed the job until his retirement in 1999.

○

Dan Jackson wrote his first ticket as the new police chief of Clear Lake, Iowa, to himself. During a television interview about his appointment, Jackson was filmed driving his cruiser, but several viewers noticed that he wasn't wearing his seat belt as required by state law. The mistake cost him $21.50.

○

John A. Greene, a doctor of psychology in Boston, earned $109,000 one year administering tests for the Massachusetts Medicaid program. He also held down a $40,000-a-year, full-time day job at the Veterans Administration coordinating a methadone treatment program. Greene also picked up another $23,000 working five nights a week for the Massachusetts Water Resources Authority, where his duties consisted of shoveling human waste. Asked why he worked at a job MWRA officials described as "one of the worst, most difficult and unpleasant jobs in state government," Greene admitted, "I honestly don't know."

OKAY, YOU EXPLAIN IT

In 1989 a woman eating a tunafish sandwich in her 31st-floor apartment in Philadelphia was hit in the arm by a bullet. Police determined that the bullet entered the apartment window on an even trajectory but there are no neighboring buildings at the same height. "We have no idea where this bullet came from," said Capt. Richard Kirchner. "If you look out, the only thing in that area that's really tall is the Arco burn-off tower," which is two miles away.

○

On September 7, 1989, thousands of bats, many dying, landed on the streets and sidewalks of Fort Worth, just prior to the evening rush hour. Jeff Derosa of the Humane Society said that he found 100 bats on the sidewalk and that at least 1,000 were hanging from the eaves of one building. One Humane Society official suggested that they may have been poisoned or were suffering from heat stroke.

A house in Orland Hills, Illinois, was ordered bulldozed in 1988 by the Travelers Insurance Co. after a battery of scientific tests failed to detect the source of mysterious flames shooting from electrical sockets and appearances of a mist and the smell of sulfur inside the house. Arson investigators Steve Smith and Terry Hyland said that tests conducted by engineers, chemists, geologists, and explosives experts all failed to come up with an explanation. Fire officials listed twenty-six separate reports of strange phenomena at the house in a six-month period. Two police officers and two engineers witnessed a flame one inch in diameter shoot 21 inches out of a bedroom wall socket and hit a mattress. "The fire was under pressure, and that kind of pressure can't build up in an electrical conduit because it's open throughout the entire house," said Smith. Both the local fire department and the Travelers Insurance Co. concluded that the house was unsafe for habitation.

Earlier that year a house in Clifton, New Jersey, exhibited similar phenomena. Between January 30 and February 10, as many as six small fires started in wall sockets and light sockets. The Public Service Electric & Gas Co. even cut off all power to the house in an attempt to find the cause. This led them to believe that the problem was not in power lines but "in the house itself." On the second day without power, firefighters responded to investigate the source of smoke that appeared in the house.

○

After the New Jersey Department of Transportation began construction on a 7.2-mile stretch of Route 55 in 1983, the following things occurred: One construction worker was run over by an asphalt roller truck; another was blown off a bridge overpass; one inspector died on the job of a brain aneurysm; one worker's feet mysteriously blackened; one worker's wife miscarried; a van carrying five workers burned and exploded; one worker's parents were killed in an auto accident the night after the project began; the brother and father of one worker died on the same weekend. Carl Pierce, chief of the Delaware Indians, said that the construction desecrated an ancient burial ground.

○

In 1988 Britain's Pauline Shaw, 46, claimed that her body was so full of electricity that her mere touch could damage household appliances. She was reported to have destroyed 25 irons, 18 toasters, 15 kettles, 6 tumble dryers, 10 washing machines, 12 television sets, 12 radios, 3 VCRs, and at least 250 lightbulbs. She said that she once damaged her bank's computer by leaning on a terminal. Doctors who examined Shaw theorized that an allergy or stress might have somehow been responsible for her condition. "It's not a party trick, something I do at will. It comes suddenly, by itself," said Shaw.

That same year, The New China News Agency reported that a Xinjang factory worker was so electrically charged that his touch could knock a person down.

○

According to a 1989 article in the British medical weekly *The Lancet*, a two-year-old dog discovered a malignant tumor on the thigh of her owner, Bonita Whitfield, 44. For several months, the dog spent a few minutes each day sniffing the tumor and sometimes tried to bite it off. Her behavior eventually prompted Whitfield to seek treatment.

○

In 1982, scientists in Australia were baffled by a mysterious spider whose poisonous venom destroyed human skin and flesh to the point that plastic surgery was needed to repair it.

Canadian chemist David Dolphin theorized in a 1985 study that legends of vampires and werewolves were actually based on cases of victims of porphyrias—diseases that involve a malfunction in the biochemical production of heme, the blood's red pigment. Such victims are extremely sensitive to the sun and can develop chemical imbalances that lead to the destruction of tissue. Dolphin suggested that some victims could develop fanglike teeth as gums were destroyed and also might become very hairy. Since heme injections are used today to treat the disease, Dolphin postulated that victims in the Middle Ages may have turned to drinking large amounts of blood for its heme content.

○

According to a report from police in Zimbabwe, a pack of baboons kidnapped 2-year-old Thomas Mazvipedza and carried him 15 miles from his home. Police said that the boy's parents consulted a medium who directed them to a hill where searchers found baboon tracks. Thomas was found asleep and unhurt but stripped naked.

IN CONTEXT

A 1986 report by a U.S. Department of Education panel on a history curriculum designed for students to react to the genocide of Jews during World War II criticized the content of the curriculum as "unfair" to Nazis and the Ku Klux Klan. The report stated, "The program gives no evidence of balance or objectivity."

○

From a tape-recorded exchange in 1983 between San Francisco Giants manager Joe Altobelli and a San Francisco sports writer with whom he had been feuding:

WRITER: [asks question]
ALTOBELLI: What is this, some f———' kind of third degree?
WRITER: I'm just asking.
ALTOBELLI: Well, f—— you. Ask that, son of a bitch. Take it for what it's f———' worth. What the f———! Christ! We win the f———' ball game 2 to 1 and you're f———' giving me the f———' third degree. Go sh— in your f———' hat. What the f———. You're trying to tell me how to f———' manage, is that right?
WRITER: I'm asking a question about why you did that.
ALTOBELLI: Oh, bullsh—. Those f———' questions are horse-sh—. That's what I think of those f———' questions.

They're f———' horsesh—. If you want to be a manager, go f———' sweat your ass off fourteen f———' years in the minor leagues. What kind of sh—? F———' horesh—. That's what it is. And tell the whole f———' world I said it. I gotta come in here and answer that kind of sh—. That's f———' tripe. Out-and-out f———' tripe. Good f———' night.

○

Hugh Hefner, on the origin of the Playboy bunny: One of Hefner's treasures as a kid was a blanket "with bunnies all over it," he said. Then he got a dog, which became sick and died and was laid out in the blanket and burned. "When the blanket went up in flames," said Hefner, "the bunny empire began."

○

Donald J. Talmont, 20, was charged with criminal damage to property after he rammed his car into ten trees and three street signs in Milwaukee on the night of a lunar eclipse in 1989. Police quoted him as saying that he only gets that way when there is a lunar eclipse.

○

Then-U.S. Representative Richard Kelly (D-Florida), who was later convicted in the Abscam scandal in the late 1970s after a videotape showed him furiously stuffing payoff money into various pockets in his coat, was quoted earlier by the *Wall Street Journal* concerning a piece of consumer regulation: "I think the free-enterprise system is absolutely too important to be left to the voluntary action of the marketplace."

○

A Florida assistant attorney general in charge of the criminal division in the early 1980s, George Georgleff, told a reporter that he knew for sure the death penalty is a deterrent to murder because visions of the electric chair once stopped him from continuing to strangle his ex-wife during a domestic dispute: "I found myself choking her, and I saw her eyes start to pop out, and suddenly off to the left or the right, I saw the electric chair."

○

Michael Angelo Vidal, Jr., 38, ran an art show in 1989 at the Burbank (California) Central Library, consisting of elaborate drawings of castles, a housing development, and the Beatles, done on Etch-A-Sketch, at prices from $200 to $500. Asked why Etch-A-Sketch, Vidal said, "I get more response out of this medium."

○

Jesse Jackson, analyzing the 1979 takeover of the U.S. embassy in Iran during a 1984 presidential campaign debate: "Now, once the crisis [takeover] struck, we could not fight back militarily. It's like a man who's dashing to get over a fence and his vital organs get trapped, and the Ayatollah has a hatchet and breathing fire—that's not a time for a quicker helicopter. You've got to fake your way out of that situation and have the patience to wait until your chance comes."

○

Writing a majority opinion for the Utah Supreme Court affirming the conviction of pornographer James Piepenburg while upholding the Utah obscenity law even though it was significantly stricter than the U.S. Supreme Court test allowed, Justice A. H. Ellett wrote that state judges who went along with the U.S. Supreme Court's standard are "depraved, mentally deficient, mind-warped queers."

OOPS

The most serious injury attributed to the December 1988 Los Angeles earthquake was a man admitted to a Burbank hospital after he mistook the tremor for an intruder and shot himself in the leg.

○

St. Petersburg, Florida, assistant school superintendent Douglas Tarrant committed suicide because he was depressed over a charge of sexual abuse filed against him by a 15-year-old girl. He left behind a videotape tearfully proclaiming his innocence.

Tarrant's suicide was unnecessary, however, because just days before, the girl had recanted her story. Authorities said they were "in the process" of having the charge dropped but had failed to notify Tarrant.

○

In Kalama, Washington, 83-year-old E. C. Boone hit a dog with his pickup truck. He stopped, and his 86-year-old wife, May Belle, got out to see how badly the animal was hurt. According to Police Chief Ron Pease, the husband "looked in the mirror and thought she was motioning for him to back up and started to back up. In the meantime, she walked behind the truck and he backed over her. She started to holler and scream, then he put it in forward to drive ahead and drove it over her [again]."

○

An 81-year-old man awaiting a routine operation at Vanderbilt Hospital in Nashville died after a hospital worker mistakenly administered liquid air freshener instead of his medication. "It was a human error," Vanderbilt spokesman Jack Kennedy said, "and we are very, very sorry about the accident."

○

Alabama prison officials threw the switch to electrocute convicted killer Horace Franklin Dunkins, Jr., but two doctors who examined him afterward found that although he was unconscious he still had a strong heartbeat. A guard in the witness room opened the door and suggested to the guard directing the execution, "I believe you've got the jacks on wrong." After reversing the wires to the electrodes on Dunkins's head, officials threw the switch again. This time the 2,100 volts did the job.

"I regret very, very much what happened," State Prison Commissioner Morris Thigpen said. "It was human error."

In Huntsville, Texas, convicted murderer Raymond Landry's execution took longer than expected when a tube from an intravenous needle began to leak, sending the lethal mixture shooting across the death chamber toward witnesses. The warden pulled a curtain across the viewing area, but for more than fourteen minutes witnesses heard doors opening and closing and finally a groan. Then the curtain was reopened, and doctors declared Landry dead.

○

A 54-year-old woman in Düsseldorf, West Germany, strangled her 15-year-old daughter to death and tried to kill herself and her 13-year-old son because a computer error by the mother's medical insurance company led her to believe that she had incurable syphilis and had passed the disease on to her children.

○

James Jerge, 45, was walking in Buffalo's LaSalle Park with a woman friend after dark when he decided to go for a swim in the long-empty Centennial Pool. He scaled a fence and dived into the pool. When he failed to return, the woman phoned for help. Firefighter Raymond Whalen, 30, arrived with a rescue squad, climbed over the fence, and dived to his death.

○

Chanel Price, 31, of Venice, California, a singing-telegram entertainer hired to perform for guests at a private St. Patrick's Day party in Malibu, arrived by helicopter. As she was getting out to greet guests, she raised her hands to wave, and the chopper's blade cut off two of her fingers.

○

When performing swordsman El Hakim asked for a volunteer from the audience in Capetown, South Africa, he wanted the person to check the sharpness of the sword's blade. Before he could explain, however, the volunteer took the sword and stabbed Hakim in the back. "I guess he just misunderstood," Hakim said afterward.

○

In Hammond, Indiana, an employee of the Northern Indiana Public Service Company, sent to disconnect a customer's service because the electricity bill had not been paid, instead turned off the power to the house next door, killing a woman hooked up to life-support equipment. The utility apologized and offered to pay the woman's funeral expenses.

○

Festivities marking the centennial of organized soccer in Hereford, England, were canceled abruptly when officials discovered the league was only 90 years old.

PUT SOME CLOTHES ON

In 1983 a 44-year-old woman waiting for a bus in Goleta, California, was accosted by a naked man carrying a white cloth belt. The man, who said nothing but had an "insane smile," hit her on the thigh with the belt and walked away.

○

Baltimore police arrested a 30-year-old man in 1983 after he was found dancing nude around the body of a dead dog in a train tunnel. The man's body was painted in white glowing paint, and he was surrounded by about thirty-five people who chanted and held torches. He said that the incident was a ritual performed by members of a local cult. The man goes by the name "Tentatively, a Convenience," and said that he is a saint in the cult "just by virtue of my deeds."

In Tempe, Arizona, a 31-year-old man was arrested for indecent exposure after standing naked in a back yard bordering on the Pepperwood Golf Course on a Sunday morning and making rude comments to the golfers.

○

A 25-year-old woman in Bossier City, Louisiana, disrupted an outdoor news conference on mosquito control in 1989 when she walked by wearing only a purple sweatband on her head. Mayor George Dement asked, "Is that a naked lady over there or is there something wrong with my eyes?" Police said that the woman was walking home from the city jail after having been booked earlier that day on a charge of public drunkenness, when she decided to undress in the rain.

○

A naked man claiming to be Jesus Christ ran along Chicago's Lake Shore Drive and jumped into the back seat of an open convertible. Said Patrolman Earl Pickett, "He stood up in the back seat, grabbed the woman's hair who was sitting between two men in the front seat, and commandeered the vehicle like a chariot." The man led ten squad cars on a high-speed chase until his car struck a lamppost. Then he jumped out and, pursued by a dozen officers, leapt over a 14-foot wall and waded into Lake Michigan, where he sank. He told his rescuer, "Read the Bible."

○

New Yorker Northern J. Calloway, 32, an actor on the television series *Sesame Street*, went on a rampage through a residential neighborhood, beating a woman with an iron rod, taking a schoolbag from a child waiting for a school bus, breaking a car windshield with a rock, smashing the plate-glass window of a house, and vandalizing the interior of another home.

"My wife and I saw the man run naked into our garage," said Douglas Wright. "I got my gun and found him in there. He had spilled a bag of white herbicide on his body, and he was rolling on the ground and running around." After Wright fired a warning shot over his head, Calloway "fell to the ground screaming" that he had been shot. "Then he jumped up and washed his face and hands in our bird bath . . . and said he was a CIA man," Wright said. As he was being taken away, strapped to a stretcher, Calloway screamed, "I'm David of *Sesame Street*, and they're trying to kill me."

○

Three naked men holding their clothes in their arms stole two pizzas from a pizza delivery man in Maryland Heights, Missouri. Police suspected that the men had attended a large party that night in the neighborhood of the robbery and had come from a swimming pool.

○

County Circuit Judge Joe McDade sentenced a Pekin, Illinois, man, Robert Norton, 65, to thirty days in jail for gardening naked in his yard. Norton, convicted six times for the same offense, said that it was his constitutional right to garden in the nude.

WEIRD WEAPONS

The Smith and Wesson Company opened a golf driving range for its employees in Springfield, Massachusetts, on October 18, 1984, but was forced to close it a week later after flocks of sea gulls began bombarding company executives, motorists, and neighbors with hundreds of golf balls they would pick up, fly up into the air with, and drop.

○

A woman in Amarillo, Texas, reported to police that a tall man pushed her into an elevator, saying, "There's nothing they can do to stop me." He then proceeded to lift her dress and smash her in the buttocks with two raw eggs.

○

Two men stole $25 from a Cincinnati restaurant armed with a cicada. They thrust the bug at the cashier, 22-year-old Marquisa Kellogg, who then fled, leaving the cash register unattended.

An intense dislike of "trolls, hippies, longhairs, vagrants, commies, and welfare recipients" apparently inspired three high school seniors in Santa Cruz, California, to begin hunting them down with a deadly homemade bazooka to run them out of town. The three admitted shooting one long-haired pedestrian, who survived.

○

In Ellington, Connecticut, a 22-year-old man was charged with robbing a 28-year-old man. The assailant was armed only with a lighted cigarette, with which he threatened to poke the victim's eye out.

○

Authorities in Wisconsin Rapids, Wisconsin, investigating the death of 30-year-old Mary Herman, said the woman was killed by a "crushing type injury" that looked like a car ran over her but left no tire marks. They concluded that an elephant was the fatal weapon and charged two animal trainers from a circus that had passed through town when the woman was killed.

○

Two men entered a coin-operated laundry in Corvallis, Oregon, and went into the rest room together. After a few minutes the manager, Roy E. Bennett, went to investigate, whereupon the men suddenly bolted from the rest room. One of them was clutching the toilet seat, which he assaulted Bennett with before jumping into a car and speeding off.

○

Steven Roy Harper was sentenced to the electric chair in Nebraska in 1979 for poisoning an Omaha man, who married Harper's ex-girlfriend, and the man's infant nephew. Prosecutors said Harper set out to commit "the first murder by cancer" by contaminating a two-quart beverage container in the man's home with a cancer-causing rocket-fuel additive.

○

Earlier that year in La Hague, France, Noel Lecomte confessed to the attempted murder of his foreman at the French Atomic Energy Commission's nuclear-waste reprocessing plant by placing three highly radioactive pieces of magnesium under the driver's seat of the foreman's car. The foreman, Guy Busin, was saved from slow death by atomic radiation only because he wrecked his car and was unable to continue driving it.

○

Jurors in Linden, Alabama, convicted 37-year-old Reginald Wayne Pope of plotting to kill his mother with a rattlesnake. Prosecutors said Pope met snake handler Keith Davis by chance at a restaurant. After asking him about the possibility of using a timber rattler to kill his adoptive mother, Pope offered Davis $300 to release a snake in his mother's house.

Frank Giovanielli, 43, of Wallington, New Jersey, admitted asking a friend to put three timber rattlers in the apartment of his downstairs neighbor because she made his life "a living hell" with complaints about noise.

In Los Angeles, Michael Thompson told police a man knocked on his door, saying he had a package for him. When Thompson opened the door, the robber whipped out a knife and opened the package to display a snake, threatening to loose it on Thompson unless he handed over his valuables. The thief escaped with $400 in cash and jewelry and Thompson's car.

CHUTZPAH

A man called Miami television station reporter Art Carlson with a "news tip"—that he had just killed his wife. Then the caller asked if he could be paid, as per the station's policy, for the tip. At first Carlson thought it was a hoax, but police found the wife's body a short time later.

○

A Cleveland woman was arrested in 1987 outside a department store with 100 items that she had just shoplifted, under her clothes. Included were a padlock, a picture kit, perfume, vacuum cleaner bags, watchbands, doorstops, numerous pens, knives, screwdrivers, batteries, ten packs of cigarettes, and thirty-four key chains.

○

Two weeks after Elliot Greenspan of Ridgefield Park, New Jersey, announced as a candidate against incumbent U.S. Representative Robert Torricelli, he was jailed for refusing to testify before a grand jury investigating credit-card fraud. Within hours, he asked a friend to call Torricelli in Washington to try to intervene on his behalf.

When the late Bhagwan Shree Rajneesh was jailed in Charlotte, North Carolina, on charges of immigration fraud, he immediately requested special food and a throne for his jail cell.

○

In 1989 Lonnie "Bo" Pilgrim, an East Texas chicken magnate, handed out blank but signed $10,000 checks on the floor of the Texas legislature during debate over worker compensation legislation in which he was interested. He denied that the checks were bribes, saying they were merely a way for him to achieve "name recognition." Texas permits such contributions on the floor during special, but not regular, sessions.

○

Gregory T. Mershad, 21, of Dayton, Ohio, angrily demanded that security employees of the Marriott Marco Beach Resort in Florida find the approximately $1,000 worth of cocaine that had been stolen from his room. After the guards found the cocaine and had Mershad sign for its return, a deputy sheriff arrested him.

○

Godfrey Nairn, 45, who was arrested for striking and killing a jaywalking pedestrian and who then fled the scene in his Maserati, subsequently filed an $81,000 lawsuit against Santa Barbara, California, officials for allegedly mishandling his car and "leaving it unprotected from the weather" after they had confiscated it.

○

Three Los Angeles people were arrested as perpetrators of a scheme that cheated insurance companies out of at least $45,000 by feigning injuries and accidents. One of the three wrote a song about the scam that, when discovered by prosecutors, was one of the most damaging pieces of evidence against the three. Among its lyrics:

S is for the settlements we work for.
C is for the claims we love to fake.
A is for the accidents we engineer.
M is for the money that we make.
Put it all together, it spells scam.
Insurance is our business, and it's all a sham.

and

Most people work with pencils or with hammers.
But we invest in policies, that's why they call us scammers.
We get into an accident and then become disabled.
We claim on all our policies so scammers we are labeled.

○

Seventy people were injured in Dacca, Bangladesh, in 1988 at several college testing centers when students demanded the right to receive outside help and to copy from other students on their final exams. Nearly 500 people were injured in similar riots earlier in the year.

MARCHING TO THEIR OWN TUNE

In 1987 California Highway Patrol officer Dave Guild stopped a car traveling 50 mph on the San Diego Freeway because its hood was open and a man was under it working on the engine. The men said that they had been having trouble with the gas pedal and that the man under the hood was keeping the engine running by working the carburetor control. Neither could understand why they were being ticketed.

While Virgil E. Johnson, a custodian at the Federal Building in San Francisco, was away on vacation, federal officers opened a tiny, locked third-floor room in the building (to which Johnson had the only key) and found a bed, a hotplate, two televisions, and a large amount of cash, checks, stocks, and bonds.

Fellow workers said that Johnson had been living in the building, possibly for as long as seventeen years. They said that Johnson was mysterious, and one described him as a "mathematical wizard" who played the stock market. Chicago Board of Trade commodity charts for platinum, gold, silver, and copper were found taped to the inside of the room's door. Another said he often saw Johnson leave the building after 6 P.M. and return later with groceries.

○

Lord Avebury, 58, a British Peer of the Realm, announced in 1987 that he would be changing his will to ensure that after his death his body would be fed to the dogs of the Battersea Dog's Home. Lord Avebury said, "I think it's a terrible waste that bodies should be buried or cremated. Anyway, it's a nice gesture to give the doggies a good meal, and it will save Battersea the cost of some dog food, too."

○

Lawson Sanner was arrested in 1968 by Athens County, Ohio, sheriff's deputies after a woman reported that the 65-year-old man was hugging and kissing trees and poles. Sanner's $32 fine was suspended with the understanding that he not break any other laws for one year.

○

Lowell Davis of Savannah, Missouri, wrote down the names of every person he ever remembered meeting since the age of 3. By the age of 83, Davis had amassed 3,487 names and filled 679 pages in a binder, recording them along with notes about each. The names are arranged in chronological order by places Davis has lived. One example: "Leonard McKnight – fond of chicken gravy."

Tass reported that two years after the nuclear reactor explosion at Chernobyl, about 100 of those originally evacuated from the area had sneaked back to their homes, despite above-normal radiation levels there.

○

A mystery man appeared in Muskegon, Michigan, in 1986 and spent at least a week giving away $5 and $10 bills on street corners and in restaurants. The man, described as in his late twenties, wearing a pinstriped suit and carrying white gloves, walked into a supermarket one day and paid up the grocery bills for two shoppers.

Another mystery man appeared in Dallas in 1989 dressed in a gorilla suit and gave away more than $6,000 in $50 bills to people he met on the street. The man said he did it because "it's a heck of a lot of fun."

○

When Brian T. Nolan of Maryland lost a parking space to a man driving an Audi, he reportedly got out of his Mercedes-Benz, walked over to the Audi, and asked the driver if he wanted to fight. When the man said no, Nolan said that he would fight himself and proceeded to punch his own face about ten times. Then Nolan asked the man if he wanted to see him hit his own daughter, aged 5, whom he had left in his car. The man again said no, but Nolan allegedly pulled her from the car and hit and kicked her. At that point, the Audi driver restrained Nolan until police arrived.

○

The Federal Aviation Administration fined Larry Walters, 33, of North Hollywood $1,500 for a July 1982 incident in which he rode a lawn chair powered by helium balloons to 16,000 feet in the sky. Walters attached forty-five 6-foot weather balloons to a lawn chair along with gallon jugs of water to use as ballast. Equipped with a BB pistol, a CB radio, and a parachute, he had planned simply to rise up into the air, keeping one ground tether intact. When that line broke, however, Walters shot up to 16,000 feet, where he was seen by TWA and Delta airline pilots. Walters called for help on his CB radio and began shooting out the balloons with his pistol. As he began to descend, some of the tether ropes pulled down power lines, blacking out part of Long Beach. His chair was eventually suspended only 5 feet off the ground, and Walters was able to jump down.

○

Ray Valine, 30, of Sacramento said that he earned $100 a day advertising various shops and services by painting their names on his shaved scalp. Valine got the idea when he shaved his head to paint it like an Easter egg. His wife did the painting. He said that his previous job as a trash collector didn't work out because his bosses gave him a "hard time" for dressing up as Santa Claus, Uncle Sam, and the Easter Bunny on holidays.

○

Hearing his front window crash, Edward Alsop of Mansfield, England, found a stone bearing a text from the Scriptures and signed, "God." Police said the sender was actually Philip Dring, self-styled preacher in the Assembly of God Congregation—a peculiar sect that allows beer drinking and smoking during services and is partial to wife swapping. Next day, six of Dring's followers stoned Alsop's windows. Investigators say they were trying to persuade Alsop to rejoin the sect. "God moves in mysterious ways," said Peter Burt, a sect member. "I knew we had to break the windows. It was God's will." Dring and his followers were fined $300 for the windows and for using threatening behavior.

After holding a SWAT team at bay for hours by firing rifle shots out the windows of his parents' house near Hattiesburg, Mississippi, a 22-year-old man walked out of the house at 1 A.M., placed the rifle by the mailbox, and announced he was going to bed. He was then arrested and ordered to undergo psychiatric tests.

GOVERNMENT

According to a *Wall Street Journal* article, 90 percent of the data transmitted from U.S. space missions (enough tapes to fill the floor space of fifty football fields) has never been analyzed and cannot be because the data can only be read by computers that are now obsolete.

○

The Central Intelligence Agency once hired a magician as a consultant to a project on behavior "to see if he could explain things people had a hard time trying to explain." Until his death in 1970, he also helped to write a manual for agents in using sleight of hand in administering drugs to unsuspecting persons. The agency had also asked him to analyze the work of a mystic who the agency said had devised a system for sending and receiving telepathic messages anywhere in the world.

○

The Food and Drug Administration established "performance standards" for various sexual devices under its interpretation of a 1976 statute. Covered were appliances such as douche kits, vibrators, scented deodorant menstrual pads, untreated menstrual tampons, and powered vaginal muscle stimulators, in addition to condoms, diaphragms, and IUDs. Said one official, "We only look at those that make therapeutic claims. We normally wouldn't go out to check vibrators unless it happened to be a slow day."

○

The Federal Aviation Administration, preparing for a test crash of a jetliner to examine its crashworthiness, ordered instrumented dummies for seventy-five seats on the plane. The first batch to arrive, all white dummies, were placed toward the front of the plane, and when the second, all-black batch arrived, the only seats left were in the back. FAA officials removed many of the white dummies and replaced them with black dummies so they would appear randomly distributed.

○

The U.S. Department of Energy spent $1.4 million sending the entire 25-pound, 8,800-page environmental impact statement on the superconducting supercollider to 16,000 citizens who had expressed interest in the project in 1988, when only the mailing of a summary of the statement was required by law.

○

The city of London, Ohio, sold its municipal garage in 1989 when officials accidentally included it in the deed for an adjacent building. City officials debated whether to buy the garage back or rent it from the new owner.

○

Congressional critics charged in 1988 that 16,000 State Department travel accounts were overdue, including Oliver North's (because of a failure to document a $695 advance of four years earlier) and that of a "Ludwig von Beethoven" (social security number 123-45-6789).

○

U.S. Customs Service inspectors in Buffalo seized as illegal a shipment of 5,000 uniform patches that had been ordered by the U.S. Customs Service for its agents to wear to celebrate the agency's 200th anniversary.

○

The General Accounting Office reported in 1988 that the Army had purchased 6,338 steam cleaners for its tanks for $15,000 each (total: $95 million) after having used commercial cleaners (cost: $2,100) for years. The new cleaners are so loud, however, they cannot be used in combat situations, and environmental regulations prohibit their use in peacetime.

○

In 1984, at the height of world concern about famine in Ethiopia, that country and the Soviet Union concluded a sports agreement in which Soviet athletic advisers would be sent to Ethiopia to help develop aerobics training programs. Tass announced that the program "coincides with an international effort to feed hundreds of thousands of Ethiopians."

GIVES ME THE WILLIES

Police in Colorado Springs in 1978 arrested a 39-year-old Army sergeant for practicing dentistry without a license and for third-degree assault. The man reportedly approached two boys in a local theater, identified himself as "Dr. Bob," and asked one if he had any loose teeth. The boy said that he had one, and the man allegedly pulled it, along with three others, all by hand, as the boys watched a Disney movie. "Dr. Bob" reportedly told the boy that he was collecting teeth. Police also suspected the man in two other tooth-pulling incidents.

Donald E. Maurice, 33, walked into a wood shop at Appalachian State University in Boone, North Carolina, and used a power saw to cut off his right hand. Maurice then placed the hand in a cabinet and walked off. Approached by students, Maurice said, "I don't want it back. Don't look for it. It has the mark of the beast on it. I did it to prevent myself from committing suicide."

The leader of a Missouri Boy Scout troop and his assistant were found guilty of assault charges for an incident that took place on a scout camping trip. The two men used a heated clothes hanger, twisted into the shape of male genitalia, to brand six boys on their arms or buttocks.

○

Police arrested a 19-year-old woman after she arrived at a hospital near Albuquerque carrying a newborn baby that she said was her own. Police later accused the childless woman of murdering the pregnant Cindy Lunn Ray, 23, and taking the infant from her womb.

○

Francisca Cruz, 44, of Los Angeles, was convicted of the murder of her landlady. Cruz and her son dismembered the body in a bathtub, then Cruz boiled the flesh, baked it in an oven, and packaged it. Her son then deposited the packages in trash cans in L.A.'s Chinatown district. He said that his mother intended it as food for the homeless in the area.

○

New York third-grade teacher John Cardinale, 39, stood on a crowded Canal Street subway platform muttering, "Push, push, push," moments before pushing a woman to her death in the path of an oncoming subway train.

○

Jia Yuli, a kindergarten teacher in Zhangjiakou, China, was arrested after punishing nine of her students by ordering them to place their hands in bowls of hot noodles. Jia called the students "lunatics" after discovering them pretending to be shish kebab vendors by skewering steamed buns on chopsticks.

In 1980 Michael Morgan, 19, was riding in a car through Charlotte County, Florida, with three recent acquaintances when the car stopped near a tree and the three challenged Morgan to climb it without the use of his artificial legs. When Morgan got out of the car, he was beaten, stabbed, and left to crawl half a mile for help.

○

On his way to a Thanksgiving dinner with his family in 1987, a 26-year-old man in Norton Shores, Michigan, stopped by the foundry where he worked and took his two sons inside to pick up his Bible. Police said that when the man came out alone, he approached a guard and said, "My kids are in the furnace." Asked if they fell in, he replied, "No, I put them in and lit it."

○

Convicted of a series of sniper shootings in Rhode Island and Massachusetts during 1986 and 1987, Russell J. Ducharme II said that he started shooting at people after shooting at street lights "got boring."

○

In the course of reporting on the beating death and mutilation of a family of Australian gray kangaroos at the Moscow Zoo, a Soviet newspaper noted that months earlier the zoo had experienced a rash of animal thefts. One thief stole a penguin, making his escape on the subway. Another man reportedly forced a small deer into a taxi to make his getaway.

○

A Cleveland teenager received a sentence of fifteen years to life in 1979 for paying an 18-year-old $60 to kill his father. Police said that the teen and his 15-year-old sister told them they wanted their father to die because "he wouldn't let us do what we wanted to do." The father's body was left in the family home for nine days while his children went on a spending spree with his cash and credit cards.

○

A human head buried in his yard and a human skull kept inside his house were just two examples of the evidence police collected from Robert Berdella of Kansas City in 1988. They were investigating the possibility that Berdella may have been linked to many missing persons cases. Police found torture devices and photos of people being tortured in his house after being tipped off by a nude man wearing only a dog collar who claimed to have escaped from the house. Berdella, owner of Bob's Bizarre Bazaar, a curio shop, had a business card that read, "I rise from death, I kill death, and death kills me. . . . Although I carry poison in my head the antidote can be found in my tail, which I bite with rage."

FRUITS OF RESEARCH

Tetsuo Sugawara, a 24-year-old student in information science at Japan's Yamagata University, died of suffocation when he taped up his nose and mouth as part of an apparent experiment to monitor the effects of breathing on body movement.

O

Rather than deter crime, highly publicized executions may actually provoke killings that never would have occurred, according to researchers William Bowers and Glenn Pierce of Northeastern University's Center for Applied Social Research. They noted that in New York state between 1907 and 1963 there were two additional homicides, on the average, in the month after an execution.

O

Mafia gangsters suffer worse stress than top business executives, according to Dr. Grancesco Aragora. After spending forty years studying mafiosi remains, the Sicilian pathologist said the gangsters tend to have thickened arteries, kidney failure, stomach ulcers, and livers that are "yellowish, fatty, and chronically short of glucose."

○

Beverly Hills dermatologist Dr. Arnold Klein reported one benefit of pollution is that it can keep your skin looking young by blocking sunlight that can age it.

○

Jesus was probably not celibate, did not advocate celibacy, and had a "special relationship" with at least one woman, according to a committee of religious scholars, led by Robert W. Funk of Westar Institute in California. The participants analyzed 758 sayings of Jesus and judged only 148 to be authentic. Among their findings: Jesus did not preach much of the Sermon on the Mount, did not predict his own death, and did not expect to return to earth. A paper by Peruvian Lutheran scholar Leif Vaage went so far as to call Jesus "a party animal, somewhat shiftless and disrespectful of the Fifth Commandment: Honor your father and mother."

○

Researchers at Georgia Tech paid volunteers $15 to tumble down a flight of stairs as part of a project to find out how a body falls.

○

The best way for a person to approach an escalator, according to research by University of California at Berkeley Professor Theodore L. Cohn, is from the side with one eye closed. He said such a strategy would prevent some of the 60,000 falls that occur on moving stairways in the United States each year.

Researchers at Langley Air Force Base, Virginia, trying to reduce accidents caused by jets hitting birds, converted a 20-foot-long cannon to fire 4-pound chickens at 700 mph into engines, windshields, and landing gear to determine how much damage such collisions can cause.

○

In 1982 Larry Rogers sat in his laboratory in Jacks Valley, California, experimenting with grain wastes and a bacterium he thought would dissolve explosive materials. It didn't work, but Rogers discovered something better—bulletproof wheat. He said his compound could be used to manufacture a broad range of products, among them lightweight armor, a wood substitute, and pasta.

○

Brad Coker, whose firm conducted a statewide exit poll in Virginia's 1989 gubernatorial election, denied that his poll's failure to project the actual closeness of the race—Democrat L. Douglas Wilder won by fewer than 7,000 votes out of 1.5 million—had anything to do with the way the poll was conducted. Instead, he blamed the 10 percent error on thousands of Republican voters he accused of deliberately lying to pollsters about the way they voted.

○

Seventy-three percent of the adults who responded to a poll by *Parents* magazine said they favored "a high level of patriotism" in the nation, but only 53 percent admitted owning an American flag.

○

Ten cows burp enough gas in a year to provide for all the space heating, winter heating, and cooking requirements of a small house, according to a study reported in *Epalog*, the official publication of the Environmental Protection Agency.

○

The Indians at the Battle of the Little Bighorn were better armed and sneakier than experts had suspected, according to an archaeologist who directed the first major excavation of the site where Lt. Col. George Armstrong Custer and about 220 soldiers were wiped out on June 25, 1876, by between 1,500 and 4,000 Cheyenne and Sioux warriors. Douglas D. Scott of the National Park Service said his dig turned up 117 Indian weapons, including 60 lever-action rifles, and from these he estimated that the Indians carried at least 350 firearms into battle.

The dig also found six positions where the Indians took cover in the grass and surrounded Custer's troops during the 90-minute battle. "There has been an assumption that the Indians just rushed in there en masse, the old Errol Flynn image of war-bonneted savages defending their territory," Scott said. Instead, it appears they cautiously crouched and picked off the soldiers, thinning their ranks before swarming in and killing those who remained.

THE ONLY WAY OUT

A 30-year-old California man committed suicide in 1980 with an overdose of drugs because, according to a suicide note, "I just can't live another four years with Reagan."

○

A 27-year-old man and his 21-year-old wife, who were likely to receive no more than probation on minor drug charges in Rockville, Maryland, committed suicide in full view of their parents and relatives by downing cyanide packets in the courtroom just before their sentencing.

○

A 17-year-old boy identified only as Eugene killed himself with a drug overdose in Sevran, France, because his parents had refused to pay for plastic surgery that would enable him to look like Michael Jackson.

Melbourne, Australia, police say a 32-year-old man committed suicide in 1989 by climbing a 4½-foot fence into a lions' den at the Melbourne Zoo, to be mauled to death by the four inhabitants. Police say it was suicide because the man was found naked, with his clothes neatly folded just outside the fence.

O

In 1989, people in Houston, Pontiac (Michigan), Miami, and Tampa committed suicide minutes after either being stopped by police for minor traffic infractions or having been involved in minor collisions.

O

Letter carrier Charles Palmer shot himself to death in Hilton Head, South Carolina, two days before his trial for mail fraud was to start. He had been accused of ordering over 300 magazine subscriptions for an optometrist as retaliation for an unsatisfactory pair of eyeglasses prescribed him.

O

Tennessee Secretary of State Gentry Crowell attempted suicide in 1989 by a shotgun blast through his mouth after allegations surfaced in a scandal over charity bingo games.

LET'S MAKE A DEAL

A shortage of kidneys for transplants in West Germany prompted Dr. Hugo Harms to begin offering $32,000 for people in Brazil and India to donate theirs. He explained the money would enable the donors to live comfortably for the rest of their lives and that he could cover his costs by marking up the price to his West German patients waiting for kidney transplants.

○

Saudi Sheik Mohammed al-Fassi offered Midland, Pennsylvania, $3 million if all the town's voters would pledge to vote against President Reagan in the 1984 election.

○

In Fitchburg, Massachusetts, someone stole a 3-foot-tall ceramic statue of the baby Jesus from the crèche set up by the Rotary Club and left this ransom note: "We have Jesus. We will hang him unless the police leave five cases of Budweiser here January 1."

Students in Stuttgart, West Germany, resorted to deliberately infesting themselves with head lice to get themselves barred from school. The German Education Ministry reported the students were paying the equivalent of $2.60 for the parasites.

○

Merchants in Roanoke, Virginia, put up a million-dollar offer to any musicians willing to create a rock band called "Roanoke."

○

In China, two brothers with a gambling addiction sold their mother to a peasant in Kwangsi province after tricking her into affixing her thumbprint to a bill of sale.

○

A husband and wife armed with shotguns in Norwich, New York, held sixteen workers hostage in the Chenango County office building for about six hours before offering to release them in exchange for the couple's two pet dogs. Larry and Christine Gladstone also demanded the return of forty dogs and cats taken from their farm a year earlier, food, and telephone contact with President Reagan.

○

John Alvin Jackson of Trenton, South Carolina, admitted giving his estranged wife to another man to settle a $200 debt because he was "red hot mad" at her. After getting her to go with him under the pretense of spending a long weekend at a lake to try to reconcile their marriage, he suggested they stop by Frank William Yeck's place in Grovetown, Georgia, to pick up a Bible. There, Jackson handed her over. Yeck placed her in bondage and forced her to participate in various sexual activities before she escaped the next day.

At Yeck's trial, she testified that she submitted to him because she feared for her life and her son's. Yeck testified that the woman was a willing participant in his actions. "If I had any idea they were against her will, I would have stopped," he said. "I showed her how to enjoy sex. Pain was the objective to a certain extent."

Johnson, who testified against Yeck as part of his plea bargain, said Yeck had assured him he would not harm her. Afterward, Jackson said Yeck told him, "It's nothing serious. The marks will go away in a couple of days. I know what I'm doing."

○

In Allegan, Michigan, a man was charged with stripping his wife and 7-year-old stepdaughter, wrapping their hands, feet, and faces in duct tape, and trying to sell them for $150 to two men who police said planned to force the woman to bear children they later would sell and to use the girl as a household slave.

○

Babies are a commodity to some parents and fetch a variety of prices, as shown by these examples from 1979 through 1989:

- A middle-aged Greek couple, Mr. and Mrs. Andreas Kontoyannis, made a career of fertility, producing sixteen children and selling fourteen to foreign buyers—$20,000 for a set of twins and between $2,000 and $8,000 for each of the other children sold.

- In a case celebrated in Elvis Costello's song "Less Than Zero," a New Jersey couple was charged with trading in their 14-month-old son for a 1977 Chevrolet Corvette selling for $8,800.

- A Pasadena, Texas, man sold his 20-month-old grand-daughter for $1,700. He originally asked for $1,500 cash and an old pickup truck, but settled for the larger cash amount.

- A couple in Fort Worth offered the woman's 3-month-old daughter for a used car to take them to Mexico.

- A Knoxville, Tennessee, couple tried to trade their new-born daughter for a 25-inch color television set.

- A Baltimore couple sold their 2-year-old daughter for $7,500.

- A Severn, Maryland, couple tried to sell their 6-week-old son for $3,500 and 3 ounces of pure cocaine. Police said the couple sold a daughter a year earlier for $5,000.

- In Houston, an unemployed man and his girlfriend sold their 5-year-old son for $5,000.

- Two couples in Fort Myers, Florida, were charged with buying two children from a destitute couple for $300 each.

- New York Port Authority police arrested a 31-year-old woman who offered to sell her 11-day-old daughter to two women in a bus terminal for $100.

- A Chicago mother traded her 22-month-old son for $50 worth of cocaine.

- A 23-year-old Kansas City woman traded her 3-month-old son for $20 worth of crack cocaine.

- A St. Paul mother sold her 3-month-old daughter and 16-month-old son to a stranger for two glasses of beer.

FETISHES ON PARADE

Tempe, Arizona, police, baiting a stakeout with women's underwear, claimed to have ended the eleven-year crime spree of the area's famous "panty bandit," who they said was David Keith Fesko, 42. In Fesko's room, police found seven suitcases and numerous boxes and trunks filled with women's underwear, each item carefully marked with the owner's name and address and the date taken. (A similarly fastidious underwear bandit was operating in Salt Lake City as this book was going to press.)

○

Postal carrier John Douglas Hansford pleaded guilty to robbery in a London suburb for snatching glasses off the faces of thirty-eight young women in a spree several years ago. "I don't know why I did it," he said. "I just fancy girls who wear glasses." A court psychiatrist said Hansford had at least five years of counseling ahead of him.

Jeffrey Hill and his wife returned from a skiing weekend in 1986 to find Richard Roe, 45, of Arizona occupying their Burbank, California, house, wearing Mrs. Hill's lingerie. Roe had rearranged furniture, emptied perfume bottles, thrown away food, and posted notes at various points in the house about President Reagan and about Sally Field.

○

In 1985 Anchorage weathered a spritzing spree of a man police dubbed "The Splasher" because he squirted a caustic acid onto the buttocks of seventeen women at malls and in the street. The acid normally takes from thirty seconds to two minutes to burn through the clothing, allowing the man to escape before the victim detects the burn.

○

Criminal charges were dropped in 1980 against a man who molested female students at the University of Southern California by painting their toenails without authorization. None of the victims would testify against the man, who typically would sit across from a female student in the library, pretend to drop a paper on the floor, and while he dropped down to pick it up, quickly paint the toenails. Police labeled him "Leonardo da Toenail."

○

A man was arrested and accused of a wave of hair-snipping crimes in South Dakota, Wyoming, and New Jersey. He allegedly would sit behind women in movie theaters, snip a braid of hair, and then dash off. Police found four shoeboxes full of snipped hair in a search of his home.

Police recovered numerous photos of people's feet from the home of Brookville, Pennsylvania, farm worker John Reed, 57, along with videotapes of parades in which the camera zooms in on marchers' feet.

○

James Phipps Davis, 35, was arrested in 1989 and charged with thirteen North Carolina church and day-care center break-ins. Among the items missing were baby bottles. When arrested, Davis was hiding in a church closet wearing disposable diapers.

○

Police in Baton Rouge reported that a man wearing a gorilla mask broke into a home and held a mother and her 18-year-old daughter at gunpoint for fifteen minutes while forcing the girl to model underclothes.

DON'T LOSE YOUR HEAD

According to New York City police, in 1983 Charles Dingle, 23, allegedly shot Anthony Cummings, 34, in the head in a topless bar Cummings owned in Queens. Dingle then forced a mortician who happened by the bar to dig the bullet out with a kitchen knife. When she failed to find the bullet, Dingle told her to cut the head off, which she did using steak knives. Dingle was later arrested in a stolen cab with the head wrapped in party streamers and stuffed in a box.

○

Miami police arrested Alberto Mesa, 23, in 1985, when he was found walking naked through a residential neighborhood carrying a woman's severed head. As police approached, Mesa screamed, "I killed her. She's the devil."

○

Karna Ram Bheel of India, known as the man who grew the second-longest mustache in the world, was found beheaded in

1988. The 1988 *Guinness Book of World Records* recorded his mustache length at 7 feet, 10 inches. He had been growing it since 1949. Police suspected that his murderer was the son of a man Bheel had killed fourteen years earlier, when he lived as a bandit.

○

Mohamed Kassim Ismail, 32, was found in Kuala Lumpur with a deep head wound and part of his brain missing. Police suspected that someone extracted the brain in a ritual sacrifice to bring good fortune in Malaysia's weekly lottery.

○

United Parcel Service employees in Louisville in 1986 noticed a leaky box and opened it up to find twelve severed human heads in plastic bags. The discovery resulted in an investigation of the business practices of a Philadelphia specialist who had apparently been mailing body parts to medical schools for fifteen years.

○

Severed heads found in 1989 included a man's head (with a gunshot wound) that washed up in the surf 13 miles north of Santa Cruz, California, and a woman's head found by a golfer looking for his ball on a golf course near Trenton, New Jersey. The latter head carried the AIDS virus. Also in 1989, the decapitated body of a woman was found on a New York City rooftop in the Washington Heights section. The head was nowhere in sight.

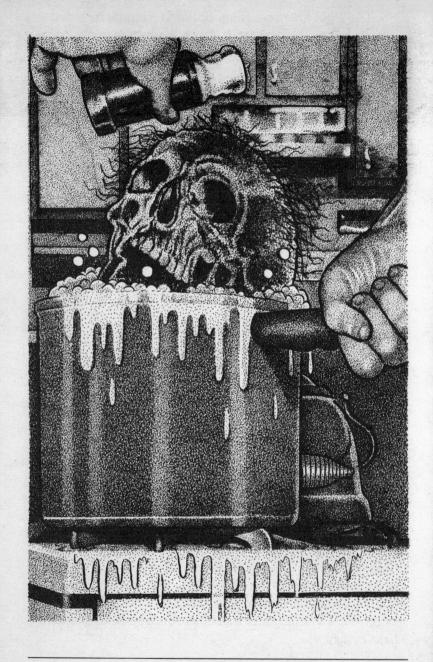

Syracuse, New York, police charged Kevin McQuain, 18, with body snatching after he was found boiling the head of a former mayor of the city on a hot plate in his dorm room. McQuain, who admitted stealing the head of Jim Crouse, dead since 1886, from a cemetery, said that he was hoping to use the skull to improve his grades in sculpting class.

MISSED THE POINT

Preston Womack of Mableton, Georgia, was arrested by Cobb County police after he sat in a restaurant wearing a pair of jockey shorts on his head and would not leave when asked. Police Sgt. M. Toler said later that "other than wearing jockey shorts on his head and socks on his hands, he was well behaved."

○

A 1982 United Nations report warned that sex education lessons were failing in certain remote Asian villages. Observers found that men were swallowing birth control pills and, to mimic the health educators' demonstrations, had placed condoms on their fingers and on bamboo poles.

○

Some recently released prisoners have not used their free time productively:

- Thirty minutes after Thomas James Rosney was released from jail in Boulder, he was arrested in the jail's parking lot for attempting to break into a car.

- Seattle police charged an 18-year-old man, who had just been released in court by Judge Philip Killien, with stealing Killien's car from the courthouse parking lot on the way home.

- Kalvin Chambers, released from Arlington, Virginia, County Jail at 12:03 P.M., on October 24, 1989, allegedly tried to steal a woman's purse on the street outside the jail at 12:17 and was back behind bars by 12:40.

○

In De Ridder, Louisiana, J. Douglas Creswell, 51, was sentenced to twenty-five years in prison in 1989 for three robberies, one of which he had botched by failing to cut eye holes in the plastic garbage bag he wore as a disguise, causing him to flail away helplessly, delaying his getaway.

○

Brian Hal Leslie, chairman of the North Miami Beach zoning code enforcement board, drew criticism in 1985 for his practice of soliciting clients for his law practice from among people who had just lost zoning decisions before his board. He advertised that he was "eminently qualified" to handle appeals. In response to criticism, Leslie said, "You know how the city is. Even if there's an appearance of conflict, they get upset."

○

A University of Maryland medical school professor was criticized for regularly prescribing the drug DES (which has been identified as a carcinogen) to retarded boys in order to stop them from masturbating in public schools when they are admitted to special programs. Another physician in the school disagreed with the therapy, saying, "There are no drugs that will stop masturbation. All it does is create big breasts in the boys."

○

John Wayne Gacy, 45, on death row in Illinois and suspected of killing thirty-three young men and boys, announced his engagement in 1988 to Sue Terry, 43, of Centralia, Illinois. Said Terry, who is the mother of eight children, of the charges against Gacy, "I don't believe hardly any of it."

NUTS BEHIND THE WHEEL

In 1989 Pope John Paul II announced two new sins: bad driving and speeding. He told Italian auto club members who attended his weekly audience that reckless drivers will have to answer to God "not only for hazardous actions that endanger one's own and other people's lives, but also for ignoring road security regulations."

○

After clearing streets for twelve straight hours, a Chicago snowplow operator stopped for dinner and a few drinks, then climbed aboard his plow and went on a rampage. After striking parked cars for several blocks, he drove onto an expressway and began hitting moving vehicles. When traffic in front of him stopped, he backed up over a Cadillac, crushing one of the occupants to death. Several other people were injured, none seriously.

"I hate my job," Thomas Blair shouted after he was pulled from the plow. "I want to see my kids. I hate my job."

As many as 100 people complained to police that the plow had struck their cars. Police discounted many of the claims, saying the plow had struck only 31 vehicles.

○

In Lusk, Wyoming, a 76-year-old woman whose license expired in December 1982 was arrested five times in the following five months for driving without a license. She had failed the eye exam required for renewal, which officials said she could have passed by wearing corrective lenses. She refused, insisting that eyeglasses were "a communist plot. Commies will land here someday and control everybody by taking away our glasses."

○

At a pretrial hearing in Mexico City for two bus drivers charged with deliberately backing over and killing a woman and a girl they had injured, Judge Jaime Gallegos pointed out that many bus companies tell their drivers to make sure they kill any pedestrians they hit because it is easier to defend charges filed by police than by surviving victims.

○

When New Jersey Transit bus driver James Coley stopped to adjust his mirror in East Rutherford, Lisa Askins pulled her Sansoria Transportation Services bus alongside and accused him of cutting in front of her. Coley denied it and continued on his route. According to riders, Askins followed and tried to force Coley off the road while the loaded buses were going about 40 mph.

When Coley, 54, finally stopped to pick up a passenger, Askins, 24, pulled in front of him, blocking his bus and three lanes of morning rush-hour traffic. She got on his bus and the two brawled until police, attracted by the traffic jam, arrived.

○

A 1986 study by Florida's Department of Transportation, noting that fatalities involving drunken bicycle riders had doubled since 1981, traced the increase to drivers who had lost their licenses under the state's tough drunken driving law and taken to riding bicycles.

○

George North of Cupertino, California, was celebrating a San Francisco 49ers' victory by riding a trash bin with rollers down an exit ramp at Candlestick Park when the bin crashed into a cement retaining wall, flipping the 39-year-old fan off an upper level of the ballpark. He fell 42 feet to his death.

○

In Los Angeles, 48-year-old Giuseppe Logreco drove his car into a dentist's office, pinning a patient against the receptionist's desk. Logreco told police he was upset because he had been trying for a month to get an appointment.

○

A Polish bus driver supposed to be carrying American journalists from Warsaw to Vilnius in Soviet-occupied Lithuania headed instead for the Ukraine. The driver explained it was the only region for which he had a road map.

LEGISLATIVE THRUSTS

When Canada's Agriculture Minister Eugene Whelen discovered that Canadian hens were laying fewer large-sized eggs recently, he ordered that "medium" eggs be reclassified as "large." Whelen is the person who told a Quebec audience that Africans have low IQs because they don't wear hats in the hot sun.

○

In 1990 for the 124th straight year, the Maryland Assembly's Committee on Investigation failed to meet.

○

Nick Sibbeston, a member of the legislative assembly of Canada's Northwest Territories, said in 1989 that the government should hire an exorcist to drive spirits from haunted houses to reduce the large real estate vacancy rates in the territories.

Singapore cracked down in 1988 on violations of its law calling the failure to flush public toilets a nuisance, punishable by a fine of up to $100 (recently raised to $500). Environmental health officers visit rest rooms at random, pretending to wash their hands but really gathering evidence.

○

Virtually all of Turkey's 51 million people stayed home on July 12, 1987, so that officials could go door-to-door drawing up new voter rolls. Police reported a surge in domestic disputes during the day.

○

The city council of Dayton, Kentucky, voted in 1974 to require Christmas carolers to obtain permits. The requirement was imposed after one group of carolers burned a woman's porch when she refused to donate money.

○

The U.S. Legal Services Corporation hired three high-powered Washington law firms to lobby Congress in 1988 to *reduce* the agency's budget by 18 percent.

○

In 1980 Harry Zain, a fundamentalist Christian and sometime political candidate in West Virginia, undertook an intensive lobbying campaign for a federal law to lower the marriage age for girls from 16 to 12. He wanted to wed his dream girl, whom he had met four years earlier in Charleston when she was 9, and in support of his proposal, visited at least sixty members of Congress at their homes in the Washington area before the FBI began encouraging him to stop.

WHEN IN ROME . . .

The barbaric tradition of the annual Gotmaar Festival continues in Pandhurna, India, despite the village's increasing modernization (10,000 TV sets among its 45,000 population). After a full moon in early September, all village activity stops, and males divide into two groups to gather rocks and then spend the rest of the day throwing them at one another, attempting to kill or injure as many as they can. At sunset, they stop, nurse the wounded, and return to normal life. In 1989, 4 were killed and 612 wounded.

○

When *M.G.*, an Indonesian music magazine, printed lyrics to the Beach Boys' "California Girls," they came out this way: "We leave those girls are in our delay . . . thing will start when they well. Meetin' in the store ground, girls with the way they talk . . . they not meet out when down bear. The mirror waste farmer's garden lately . . . make you fell all right."

An appeals court in Belgium ruled that an archery club in Zaffelare could continue the traditional sport of firing arrows into boxes of rats placed on high poles.

○

Spain's Association for the Defense of Animal Rights called on fellow Spaniards to support a demand to add cruelty to animals to the country's penal code. Among the practices they wanted outlawed was a custom at a Mardi Gras fiesta in Villanueva de la Vera in which the town's fattest man rides an old donkey until it collapses. Then it is yanked to its feet by pulling on ropes around its neck. When it is exhausted, youths join the fat man in jumping on it until it dies. Other practices it sought to stop included hurling drunken bulls off cliffs, stoning roosters, and decapitating live chickens.

○

In 1988 a witch doctor in Swaziland killed an 8-year-old child because he learned that the boy was "very clever" and wanted to use his body to make potions. The child's aunt had agreed to lure the boy to his death for $40 but alerted police after receiving only $18.

○

At least 1,786 Indian brides were murdered by their husbands or their husbands' families in 1987 because their dowries were found to be too small. It has been illegal to demand a dowry as a condition of marriage in India since 1961.

○

British authorities initiated a nationwide search in 1988 for a missing 6-year-old boy, Bernard Ward, who was believed to have been abducted by gypsies. Bernard was the seventh son of a seventh son and his father died before he was born—the two factors occurring together, in gypsy folklore, are thought to endow a child with special psychic powers.

○

Zulu chief Valindaba Ngcobo of Mafunze, South Africa, demanded compulsory virginity examinations for every girl in his domain in 1979 in an attempt to curb immorality. He asked for the elder women of each village to present him with a list of virgins, saying that he would award a bull to the village with the longest list. Any young woman found to be "deflowered," as he put it, would be made to pay an $11 fine to the chief.

○

Kawasaki, Japan's Wakamiya Hachiman Shrine, is the site of the annual "festival of the steel phallus," which commemorates a legend of an afflicted metal worker who is told by a deity to fashion a steel phallus for himself. At the festival, artisans forge a metal phallus, and participants are encouraged to design their own costumes appropriate to the celebration's theme.

○

Karnataka, India, Public Works Minister H. M. Chennabasappa told the state legislature in 1974 that his political enemies had hired witches and sorcerers to kill him. Chennabasappa, a well-respected leader of his party, trembled as he told the House that his life was in danger and that opponents had enlisted the aid of black magicians from neighboring Kerala State, reportedly the home of Hindu and Moslem sects still practicing ancient ritual magic. While the state's chief minister ordered senior police officials to find the sorcerers, Chennabasappa's friends urged him to turn to Kerala priests specializing in exorcising evil spirits. Among rumors that swept the state was that a flying skull appeared in Chennabasappa's bedroom.

○

A Thai singer was charged with killing a Laotian customer at the Thai Town Restaurant in Los Angeles in 1985 after he thought the customer had pointed the soles of his feet at him while he performed at the restaurant. Police Officer Woody Saeaee of the Los Angeles Police Department Asian Task Force said that in some Asian cultures anything having to do with feet can be insulting because the foot "is the lowest part of the body."

○

In June 1988, the Paramilitary Bangladesh Rifles arrested three people for attempting to take sixty men, women, and children across the border into India, where, according to Major Kazi Mujahid, the women would be sold to brothels and the children would be killed so their kidneys could be used in transplants. Bangladesh officials said that border guards rescued more than 2,000 people from similar fates in the first six months of 1988.

THANKS FOR NOTHING

The town of Grantham, New Hampshire, which had two streets named Stoney Brook, changed Stoney Brook Drive to Old Springs Drive and Stoney Brook Lane to Old Springs Lane.

○

Chinese soldiers burned 20 tons of used clothing donated from abroad on November 12, 1985, kicking off two weeks of officially sponsored burnings of donated foreign clothing.

○

Henri Berard of Vancouver, British Columbia, was driving home one evening when he saw a car with no lights weave through a stop sign. Berard made a U-turn and sped off to find a police officer.

He found one, but after listening to Berard's story, the cop asked for his license because he had clocked him speeding. When Berard couldn't produce his license, he was ticketed for speeding ($35 fine), driving without a license ($35), and failing to produce a license ($15). When Berard went to the police station to complain about his treatment, he was slapped with another $15 fine for overdue parking tickets.

○

Thomas Tyrrell, 35, a multiple sclerosis victim who walked from Detroit to Washington, D.C., in 1984 to dramatize the need for more research, was standing on the lawn of the U.S. Capitol, where he planned to explain his crusade to Congress the next day, when two men approached, knocked him down, hit him in the stomach, and demanded money. After Tyrrell stood up and gave them the $55 he had, one of the men kicked him in the groin while the other broke his crutch.

In a similar incident, Maria Rogers Johnson announced she was going to raise money for the homeless by walking from Peoria, Illinois, to Washington, D.C. She quit trekking after 130 miles because people along the way had contributed only $1.12. "I always believed in the goodness of people," Johnson said. "I really don't believe that anymore." She admitted that publicity about her walk didn't help, either, by revealing her criminal convictions for felony arson, retail theft, and fleeing and eluding police. The revelations also prompted her employer to fire her.

○

Southeastern Louisiana University, which dropped football in 1986 for financial reasons but decided to field a team in 1990, hired Wally English in August 1988 to coach the team, then fired him three months later for "philosophical differences," according to athletic director Bob Brodhead. "Wally English is a fine technical coach," Brodhead said, "but we need more of a public relations man, a salesman, since we aren't playing for two more years."

A 22-year-old female cab driver in San Francisco who was raped at gunpoint in her cab was fired for not screening her customers carefully enough. "I can't afford to take any chances," her boss, Guey Wong, told her in front of a reporter. "I'm lucky the cab wasn't hurt. You might endanger my insurance, you might increase my rates."

○

In Laurel Park, North Carolina, a 25-year-old man was charged with the ax murder of his mother a month after she posted $10,000 to bail him out of jail on a charge of killing his stepfather.

○

Firefighters in Moraga, California, pulled a man from a caved-in trench in a three-hour rescue that went off without a hitch— until the state Occupational and Safety Health Administration cited the fire department for violating safety regulations during the rescue. One citation related to the fact that the victim was rescued from a trench 12 feet deep. State regulations say all California workers, including firefighters, are not to go into a trench deeper than 5 feet unless its walls are shored by "metal-to-metal screw jack shorings."

"This was an emergency situation," Assistant Fire Chief Ed Lucas said. "What were we supposed to do, let the man sit there while we go find shoring from some unknown place that meets every code?"

○

Yoon No Yoon, a 31-year-old janitor from Korea accused of trying to rape a 23-year-old student in Los Angeles, cut off one of his fingers and offered it to the victim as an apology. Police recovered the finger, gift-wrapped in a box.

Residents of several drought-plagued communities in the San Francisco area in summer 1977 embraced rationing with such enthusiasm that water districts suffered significant revenue losses and were forced to relax penalties and restrictions to induce consumers to use more water—despite warnings by state authorities that the shortage was still just as serious as ever. Charles Shoemaker, assistant director of the state Department of Water Resources, accused the water districts of being "irresponsible" and "counterproductive" and warned they "could get to a point where they have lots of money but no water."

○

Randy Myer, city public information director of Lexington, Kentucky, paid $400 for a set of steel-belted tires designed to be bulletproof, bombproof, and spikeproof, then he had a flat after running over a ballpoint pen. "It still wrote," Myer said.

JUST CAN'T SAY GOODBYE

In 1985, police in Escondido, California, said that Arthur Armbruster had the body of his 87-year-old mother in a wooden box in his van and that he was driving around with it for weeks looking for the perfect burial site. Armbruster, who had buried and exhumed her body twice, said that he had "visions" that the first two burial sites were not suitable. "He's been driving around 'Mom' long enough," said detective Joe Santibanez. "I think that 'Mom' is going to have to be taken away from him."

○

Myra Joyce Vickers, 53, of Gainesville, Florida, was charged in 1989 with not reporting a death, after the body of her mother, Clara Whiting, who may have been dead for ten years, was found fully clothed under a blanket on her couch. An anthropologist who autopsied Whiting's body said that it did not consist of much more than skeletal remains.

○

The body of William P. J. White, 82, of Millsboro, Delaware, was found at home in bed about three years after his 1980 death. Police discovered the body after responding to an inquiry by a neighbor who "hadn't seen the gentleman for a couple of years and . . . hadn't heard about a funeral." White's family believed that he was possessed by a spirit.

○

Hoping for a miracle treatment to revive their 30-year-old daughter, the parents of the diabetes victim kept her body in a bedroom for ten months, rubbing it down with a boric acid solution to preserve it. Belgian police discovered the body in 1989 after a tip from the couple's son-in-law.

○

Police in Vinita, Oklahoma, found the body of Cathy Krouse, 90, in the home of her 74-year-old son, Virgil Banks, in 1989, four years after her death. Krouse was lying in a tar-sealed coffin with an air vent. Her last wish was reported to be, "I don't ever want to leave this house."

○

John Parks, 65, of Houston, was found shot to death next to the mummified body of his 89-year-old mother, which he kept

in a rocking chair at least one year after her death. Parks apparently shot himself within days of a visit by a social worker trying to check on his mother.

◯

Carole Stevens of Knoxville, Illinois, said that she tended the mummified corpse of her husband Carl of nine years after his death because "something deep inside of me said" that he was not dead. Stevens said that she detected a "sporadic" heartbeat in Carl seven years after his death. Dentist Richard Kunce, a former guest of Stevens', who was charged with helping Mrs. Stevens forge a power of attoney to refinance her house, said, "Carl was happy and content." According to an investigator, "Kunce said he was working out . . . walked into the bedroom and Carl said, 'Good workout, Richard.' "

ORDER IN THE COURT

Edna Evon Sims filed a lawsuit in Columbia, South Carolina, against the maker of two hair-care products after a 1988 incident in which, while standing at a bus stop on a 96-degree day, her hair suddenly burst into flames. A passing police officer moved quickly to put out the fire, but Sims claimed to have suffered permanent disfigurement.

○

Milwaukee County Circuit Judge Clarence Parrish could have given a ten-year sentence to the man before him after an admission that the man had had sex with his 12-year-old stepdaughter and had fathered two children by another stepdaughter, but the judge awarded him only probation (for 4½ years) because he thought the man was God-fearing. Parrish had asked the man during sentencing who was the author of the Book of Revelation, and the man's correct answer ("John") may have swayed the judge.

Professional psychic Judith Richardson Haimes won more than $1 million from a Philadelphia jury because, she said, a faulty CAT scan at Temple University Hospital robbed her of her ability to see the future. When a Temple lawyer announced after the trial that Temple would appeal, Haimes incorrectly predicted that Temple would lose that appeal.

○

When shooting victim Kenneth Donaldson was asked to walk about a Detroit courtroom and "identify" his alleged assailant from among courtroom spectators, he wandered until his eyes fixed on a man in the last row. He said, "That's him," then reached over two seats and slugged the man in the face. The prosecutor then said, "I ask that the record reflect that the complainant has just identified the defendant."

○

Gary Begley, 45, filed a lawsuit asking $180,000 from the Worldwide Church of God in Los Angeles, claiming damages from the church's preaching to him over the years to abstain from sex. He asked $30,000 per year for the six years between the time of divorce until the church finally relented and allowed a divorced man to remarry.

○

Jimmie Perko and Neil Sleeper, inmates who broke out of the medium-security Moberly (Missouri) prison before being rearrested, filed a $1.8 million lawsuit against the state because they claimed the reason they had to escape was that it was too dangerous in prison and that the state refused to protect them. According to the lawsuit, "a person can only put up with this constant fear for so long until he is forced to seek safety." As evidence of the prison guards' negligence, the men reminded the court that the guards had failed to detect the two men "tearing the window out of their cell."

○

Terry and Deborah Shook sued the city of Pawtucket, Rhode Island, for $115,000 because their son's second-grade teacher forced him to lick saliva off the playground during recess as punishment.

○

Patricia Tinerella, 25, was awarded $2,660 in back pay from her Omaha employer for a 1983 incident in which she was fired. The firm claimed she performed inadequately, but the state equal employment opportunity commission found that she was fired because her 40-inch bust distracted co-workers and that she had declined to follow her employer's suggestions on how to deemphasize what the commission called an "immutable characteristic."

○

According to testimony by a psychiatrist, the plaintiff in an exploding-bottle lawsuit against Coca-Cola in 1980 in Nashville said that she had had nightmares in which "giant" Coke bottles "marched" toward her and then exploded when they got close. The plaintiff, a former real-estate agent, said she had dreamed that a real-estate sign with her name on it once changed into a large Coke bottle and chased her.

○

A court in Tel Aviv ordered a 16-year-old girl to stop walking around her house naked after complaints by her 80-year-old stepfather. The man accused her and her mother of trying to induce him to have a heart attack so they could inherit his fortune.

○

A 32-year-old Sacramento woman sued Dr. Eugene Zavri and a local hospital because a piece of equipment accidentally lodged in her throat after it broke off during surgery in 1978. She coughed it up three days after the operation but continued to have the sensation that something was lodged there when it wasn't. As a result, she contended in the lawsuit, she was unable to perform oral sex. "She states she's had to modify her usual sexual techniques and that this makes her feel deprived because she is not able to give her partner the joy and pleasure that she thinks is his due," according to the lawsuit.

LAST DAYS OF THE PLANET

In a 1988 ABC-TV poll of 17-year-olds, one girl answered that the Holocaust was "that Jewish holiday last week, right?" Another thought the Ayatollah was a Soviet gymnast, and yet another thought Chernobyl was Cher's full name.

○

A sex educator told a Florida House of Representatives committee in 1989 that some high school boys were playing a game in which the winner would be the one who fathers the most children during the school year.

○

Forewarning of a decline in morality, civic leaders and parents in Addis Ababa, Ethiopia, had to quell a fad in 1986 in which children banded together dressed as Michael Jackson, mimicked his movements, and marauded through the city and suburbs causing disturbances. Boys were wearing rouge and lipstick.

○

A 1987 *Philadelphia Inquirer* story on colleges' spring break in Ft. Lauderdale reported on a stupid-tricks contest in which contestants flouted national concern over the spreading of AIDS. In one, six men from Penn State brushed their teeth in turn, with the second using the discharge from the first's brushing, until the sixth man drank the remainder. Holy Cross was the crowd favorite, the newspaper reported, for a stunt in which one student vomited into the other's mouth. Said the master of ceremonies, "We're all here to have fun."

○

Graduation exercises were canceled at Fairview (Pennsylvania) High School in 1988 because of fears that several students might try to commit suicide on stage.

○

A survey of 1,500 Australians released on International Women's Day in 1988 revealed that one-fifth of Australian men believe it is acceptable to kick or beat a wife if she disobeys or fails to keep the house clean. And a Rhode Island Rape Crisis Center survey in 1988 revealed that 24 percent of seventh- to ninth-grade boys and 16 percent of the girls believe it is acceptable for a man to force a woman to have sex if he has spent money on her. The figures went up to 65 percent and 47 percent if the couple had been dating for six months or more.

The Army called the Divad anti-aircraft cannon "the most so-phisticated piece of equipment ever to roll onto a battlefield" at its unveiling to press and military brass in 1982. The ma-chine was later revealed not to be able to hit a maneuvering aircraft, not to work in the rain or at night, to send out a ra-dar signal so strong that it was impossible to cover it up, and to aim less effectively than the human eye. At its unveiling, the "brain" caused the cannon to swing uncontrollably away from the target and toward the reviewing stand, forcing the brass to duck for cover.

○

Thailand's wildlife conservation director Pramoj Saivic warned in 1986 that his country's last herd of wild elephants (around 2,000) was in danger of extinction from hunters' seeking the males' penises for making Chinese aphrodisiacs. The penises weigh around 44 pounds and sell for about $10 a pound. They are smoke-dried according to China's traditional pharma-copoeia.

○

Former astronaut Rusty Schweikart, serving as a science ad-viser to then-Governor Jerry Brown of California, was used as a prop at an antinuclear demonstration at a "World Sympo-sium on Humanities" in Pasadena. Dancers carrying drums and tambourines surrounded the panel on which Schweikart was speaking, affixed metal stars to the foreheads of Schweikart and the other panelists, and chanted antinuclear slogans. Schweikart told the dancers, "I love you," and told the audience that "ev-ery one of us is both evil and good, wrapped in this one thing."

WEIRD CO-INCIDENCES

In Draperstown, Northern Ireland, 67-year-old Charles Rogers was watching a grave being dug for his dead brother when the sides started to cave in. Rogers reached down to help a gravedigger and fell in himself, followed by the headstone, which crushed and killed him.

○

Jessie G. Ziegenhagen, 35, was driving through a crime-ridden neighborhood in Hollywood, Florida, showing a friend how bad the area had become when a man ran from a building and fired a shot that hit Ziegenhagen in the head, killing him.

○

A five-man gang rushed into a Robert Hall clothing store in Indianapolis and announced a holdup—only to discover that another five-man gang was already there, staging a robbery. When someone fired a gun, both gangs began grabbing clothes

The World's Smallest Man

The World's Smallest Man

off the racks and fled. City police detective Sgt. Harry C. Dunn nabbed one of the gangs after spotting a car with five of the suspects and gave chase as the occupants flung clothing out the window. The other five escaped.

○

Visitors to the Kentucky State Fair in 1980 encountered two men claiming the same title. Ricki Donovan, 35 inches high, billed himself as the "world's smallest man." Down the midway, also billed as the "world's smallest man," was Pete Moore, 28 inches high. In spite of the obvious discrepancy, Donovan refused to relinquish his title.

○

Two sisters who hadn't seen each other since childhood were reunited—in jail. The women, Joyce Lott, 27, and Mary Jones,

29, met in the Women's Correctional Center in Columbia, South Carolina, where both were doing time on drug charges. After a newspaper printed a story about their reunion, they received a call from Frank Strickland, who said he was their long-lost half-brother. He explained it would be a while before he could come to see them since he was in jail, too, on drug, burglary, and larceny charges.

In a similar case, Robert Arthur Magoon and his father Michael Arthur Magoon, estranged since the son's birth, were reunited after nineteen years when both turned up as inmates at the Santa Clara County, California, jail, the son for violating parole and the father for robbery.

○

One group that responded to an appeal to donate clothing to survivors of the December 1988 earthquake in Armenia was the Potomac Rambling Bares, a Washington, D.C., area nudists' club.

○

A student in an anatomy class at the University of Alabama School of Medicine in Birmingham informed the school's director that one of the cadavers being dissected in the class was her great aunt.

○

Kenneth Wiggins, 45, was driving to work in St. Clairsville, Ohio, when his car apparently crossed the center line and slammed into a car driven by his wife, Nancy, 41, who was on her way home from work. Both were hospitalized in fair condition.

In Elmwood, Wisconsin, Jean Bechel, 19, was hospitalized in fair condition after her car collided with a car driven by her twin sister, Jan, who suffered minor injuries.

Dallas city councilor Roland Tucker, known as a crusader for crime prevention, had his parked car stolen after leaving the keys in the ignition. The car contained Tucker's research material on crime prevention, including information pertaining to a proposed ordinance making it illegal to leave the keys in the ignition of an unattended car.

THE VOICES IN MY HEAD

James P. Riva, 24, of Brockton, Massachusetts, a self-professed vampire, was convicted for the 1980 murder of his grandmother. Riva shot her with gold-tipped bullets and tried to drink her blood. Janet Jones, Riva's mother, testified that her son told her, "I've been a vampire for four years. Voices told me I had to be a vampire and I had to drink blood for a long time. I've been talking with the devil for a long time." The bullets were tipped with gold paint because vampires told him that they "would find their mark." Jones also said that Riva believed that a transmitter had been placed inside his head by a spaceship and that the transmitter directed his body. Occasionally he wore a cardboard pyramid over his head, according to Jones, because it "fixed his brains."

○

Barend Strydom, a 23-year-old ex-police officer in South Africa, went camping and meditated for three days before going on a shooting spree that left seven blacks dead. Strydom said that he prayed to determine if Jesus Christ approved of his mass murder plans and took the fact that Jesus did not appear to him as a sign of approval. Strydom testified at his trial that he would repeat his actions if freed.

○

A member of the Outlaws motorcycle gang in Tennessee, Arthur Gary Voltz, confessed to the murder of his go-go dancer girlfriend, saying that he was a German general and that when he killed her he was acting on orders. A truck driver testified at the trial that he was parked along I-40 the night of the murder when Voltz approached him and said that he needed orders to kill someone.

○

Michael Trofimov pleaded not guilty by reason of insanity in the murder of his father. Trofimov, who had recently joined a religious group, was found with his hands around his father's neck "speaking in tongues and screaming for God." His uncle said, "He was a good young man and then he started going to these [religious] meetings." His uncle also noted that the night before the murder Michael apparently drove his car into a train and that that "really triggered him off."

○

The jury at Thomas Lee Bonney's trial for the 1987 murder of his daughter Carol Bonney in North Carolina watched videotapes of the defendant assuming the voices of multiple personalities while hypnotized. A psychiatrist diagnosed ten separate personalities in Bonney. The one known as "Satan" said, "I know everything. I am strong . . . I control Tom. He's dumb . . . a wimp . . . a goody-goody, talking that Jesus garbage all the time." On the night of her murder, Carol and her father argued over a love letter to a boyfriend whom "Satan" called "that stupid newt." "Satan" then noted that Carol "called [me] a bastard. She sorta goofed when she called [me] that."

○

Kenneth Erskine, 24, accused of strangling seven elderly people in England, claimed that a whispering woman's voice came out of walls and doors, caused dizzy spells, and tried to control him. "It tries to think for me, it says it will kill me if it can get me, it blanks things from my mind," Erskine told a police detective.

○

Police said a 36-year-old father in Little Rock, Arkansas, beat his five children (aged 4, 6, 7, 8, and 11), held their heads under water, and forced them to smoke crack cocaine because "God told him to do it."

○

Ned Searight brought suit for $14 million against the State of New Jersey in 1976, charging that while in custody in 1962, the state unlawfully injected him with a radium electric beam. Searight claimed that as a result of the injection, someone talked to him on the inside of his brain. The case was dismissed by the United States District Court on the grounds that the suit was barred by the statute of limitations. In his opinion, the judge noted, "But taking the facts as pleaded . . . they show a case of presumably unlicensed radio communication, a matter which comes within the sole jurisdiction of the Federal Communications Commission. . . . And even aside from that, Searight could have blocked the broadcast to the antenna in his brain simply by grounding it. . . . Searight might have pinned to the back of a trouser leg a short chain of paper clips so that the end would touch the ground and prevent anyone from talking to him inside his brain."

Mario Arballo filed a $20-million damage suit charging former *Charlie's Angels* actress Jaclyn Smith with sexual torture. Arballo claimed that the torture began March 27, 1977, when he was watching a muscular dystrophy telethon and Smith appeared on screen. Arballo said that Smith immediately began to torture him with telepathic messages containing suggestions for "deviant sexual acts" that continued well after the telethon ended.

WEIRD CLERGY

In 1983 an 18-year-old student at Colorado State University alleged that a Fort Collins Catholic priest threw her down a flight of stairs because he was upset at her tambourine playing during Mass. She quoted him as saying, "You play the same way over and over again. You're not going to play at the 5:15 Mass anymore." He then grabbed her by the neck and belt and threw her out the door, where she tumbled down the stairs. When the church's youth director tried to intervene, the priest slugged her in the face.

○

A storefront "church" in Greenwich Village in New York City was luring converts to its teachings in 1988 by offering as the communion drink a legal LSD-like drug. The Temple of the True Inner Light administered dipropyl tryptamine, a powerful psychedelic.

Members of America's largest Tibetan Buddhist sect demanded the resignation of its leader, Osel Tendzin, 45, in 1988 after news got out that he had contracted AIDS and had knowingly spread it to his male sexual partners. A church official said Tendzin had spread the disease to "many, many" people.

○

A *National Law Journal* article in 1988 revealed there have been more than 140 reported instances, in 18 states, of priests molesting children and that a report to the U.S. Catholic Bishops estimated that the church's liability in lawsuits by the victims could reach $1 billion over the next decade.

○

Sister Franziska Leske, 57, a Roman Catholic nun, was fined $500 in Graz, Austria, in 1988 for strangling a kitten to death with a cord after it meowed too loudly in the convent.

○

A Brownsville, Texas, jury awarded Steve Woolverton $500,000 from the local Catholic diocese for its negligence in refusing to stop Sister Mary Kregar from seducing and carrying on an affair with Woolverton's wife, a guitar player in the choir Kregar directed.

○

Grand Rapids, Michigan, Baptist minister Dwight Rymer used electric shocks to help him teach the Bible to children. He asked for young volunteers to sit on a stool wired to a 6-volt lantern battery in order to demonstrate that sometimes God "can shock you into hearing His word."

Dr. G. William Pollard, an Episcopal priest and author of *Let's Talk About Theology and Nuclear Energy*, says that nuclear power is part of God's plan and thus is essential to life. According to Pollard, one cannot both accept that God is the divine creator of all things in the universe and reject nuclear energy.

○

Los Angeles minister R. L. Hymers, Jr., asked parishioners to pray that U.S. Supreme Court Justice William Brennan would die, so that an anti-abortion justice could be appointed in his place.

FELONIOUS FOOD

London police investigating the death of 56-year-old Leslie Merry, who was fatally injured by a turnip thrown from a passing car, said the attack apparently was carried out by a gang whose members toss vegetables at random at passersby. Investigators noted that three months before Merry's death, another man suffered stomach injuries when he was hit by a cabbage.

○

Another Londoner, Ernest Coveley, pulled off fourteen robberies with cucumbers, which he wrapped in a plastic bag and waved like sawed-off shotguns to fool cashiers. After twelve of the holdups, Coveley ate his weapon in a sandwich.

○

In California, officials at the Orange County Jail refused to serve chili peppers to Hispanic inmates demanding the right to hot, spicy food. The authorities said the peppers could be used as weapons.

A woman working at the Fresh Vegetable Packing Company in Denver filed assault charges against a co-worker who hit her in the stomach with a 4-inch carrot. Police reported the attack culminated a month-old feud that began, the victim said, when the attacker hit her with a piece of fruit.

○

Two men almost bungled a robbery at a convenience store in De Ridder, Louisiana, when the one with the gun dropped it. They were able to make their getaway when one grabbed a can of carrots and started hitting store owner Clyde Hunt on the head with it.

○

The Anaheim, California, City Council banned tortilla throwing at Anaheim Stadium after some stadium patrons complained of being hit in the head by flying tortillas.

○

Police in Salt Lake City arrested a 31-year-old man who admitted robbing a check-cashing business by placing a paper bag on the counter and telling the cashier it contained a remote-controlled bomb. After handing $2,500 to the bandit, who fled, the clerk peeked into the bag and found an 18-ounce jar of peanut butter.

○

A 37-year-old man in Cleveland Heights, Ohio, took a cab to a branch of Broadview Savings and Loan and told the driver to wait while he went inside. The man told a teller that the brown leather attaché case he was holding contained a bomb. The teller gave him $2,400. The man got back into the cab, but the police pulled it over minutes later and arrested him.

When members of the bomb squad went to dismantle the bomb, they found a package of hot dogs wrapped in foil, with wires leading to a wad of putty.

○

A 34-year-old Cincinnati man, arrested for sexually attacking two women, was accused of luring the women to his apartment with promises of a gourmet dinner, then giving them drug-laced spaghetti to knock them out before he assaulted them.

○

Cisco, Texas, Police Chief Billy Rains was taken hostage by a prisoner he thought had a derringer in his back. The weapon turned out to be two pieces of beef jerky wrapped in a bread wrapper. "It felt like a real gun," Rains insisted after the forty-minute ordeal.

REACHED THE BOILING POINT

A few years ago, Miss North Carolina contestant Debbie Shook flew into a rage when informed by officials that her local title had been taken away because she had complained that she had not gotten all the prizes promised her. When the news was broken to her at the state pageant, she crushed her crown into a ball and hurled it across the stage in full view of photographers.

○

A 30-year-old woman was accused by Oakland police of shooting her husband in 1989, after tailing him on a freeway and pulling alongside his car. Police say that the incident started earlier in the evening when the husband rolled a gutter ball while bowling, causing them to lose by six pins to another couple.

A 21-year-old woman, described as smart and pretty, who was president of her high school class and of the local Future Farmers of America, and who, according to a friend, "never swore" and "never got mad at anything," was charged with killing the girlfriend of the young farmer who was her ex-boyfriend, in Wittenberg, Wisconsin.

○

Jay Halaise was arrested in Miami in 1985 when, apparently because he had been rejected by a woman in a singles bar, he cut down several utility poles with a chain saw, causing 2,000 homes to lose electricity in Coconut Grove.

○

At least three people were killed and thirty wounded in battles in central Burma in 1988 that started when a bakery worker flicked a rubber band at a Buddhist begging on the street. Demonstrators destroyed the bakery and attacked homes belonging to relatives of the owner.

○

Patricia Ridell grew tired of waiting to be admitted to the emergency room at the Westerly (Rhode Island) Hospital following a car accident. She leapt off the stretcher on which she had been waiting and drove off in an ambulance. After a chase with police, she slammed into a tree, totaling the ambulance.

○

A 13-year-old boy pulled a loaded .357 Magnum on his teacher because the teacher had refused to publish a photograph in the La Crescente, California, junior high yearbook of the boy wearing his "Anarchy Now" T-shirt.

Kansas District Judge C. Philip Aldridge of Pawnee County resigned in 1989 following an outburst over the new courthouse telephone system, which required him to punch in a personal code before making a long-distance call. Frustrated that he couldn't get a call through, Aldridge systematically attacked his phone and eight others in his suite with a saw and presented the mess to the county commissioner, along with a check for the damages and his letter of resignation.

○

Professor Arnold Arias of Chaffey College in San Bernardino County, California, was taken to a psychiatric ward after a final-exam incident in his class. Apparently upset that his classroom door was momentarily locked, Arias later marched through the room carrying an American flag and reciting the Pledge of Allegiance while students were taking the exam.

THEIR 15 MINUTES

Engineering consultant Ed Graf was hired during an emergency by Daly City, California, in 1971 to repair a sewage-line leak that was contaminating a nearby beach. Using a technique he had used in a Missouri lead-mine leak, Graf stopped the leak by stuffing in sixty Kotex sanitary napkins.

○

Pittsburgh councilman William R. Robinson proposed a leash law for cats, calling felines vicious animals known to "suck the breath out of a child" when they smell milk on the child's lips. Local veterinarians disputed the basis for the statement, despite Robinson's insistence that critics "look at all the incidents" in which a cat has sucked the breath out of a child.

○

The three children of Marion, North Carolina, street preacher David Strode (Duffy, 11, Pepper, 7, and Matthew, 6) were suspended from school repeatedly during fall 1988 for preaching hellfire and damnation, disrupting their classes in school. Especially galling to school officials was their use of words like "adulterer" and "fornicator." The father said the family does not attend church because traditional ministers are "compromising cowards." "Besides," he said, "no church will have us."

○

R. Leonard Vance, director of health standards for the Occupational Safety and Health Administration, told a committee of Congress in 1986 that he could not turn over logbooks involving allegedly improper meetings he might have had with industry representatives because his dog had thrown up all over them.

○

Brooklyn real-estate tycoon John LaCorte, 78, offered to pay $1,000 to any girl who guards her virginity until age 19, but then had to revise the plan somewhat when gynecologists contacted by reporters pointed out that obtaining proof of virginity would be impossible.

○

Richard Adams, running for the Arizona House of Representatives in 1986, admitted that he had been avoiding paying postage for years by saving envelopes he had received in the mail, inserting his own mail in them, then marking "return to sender" and dropping them back in the mail. His practice came to light when he followed the procedure when answering a mail survey by the *Arizona Republic* newspaper. He claimed that he did not know the practice was illegal.

○

An 89-year-old man in Karlsruhe, West Germany, gave the city $40,000 and promised $560,000 more if the city would erect a statue of small boys participating in a urination contest (for distance). He withdrew the offer when he did not like the initial design.

○

Kevin Kuhn, 2, was listed in fair condition after being attacked at a shopping mall in Mansfield, Ohio, by Fluffy, a 350-pound Himalayan black bear on exhibit there. Apparently Fluffy was attracted by the smell of popcorn on Kevin's face.

○

Ed Bailey was watching a football game in his home in Montana's Rocky Mountains in 1984 when he noticed a bighorn sheep staring in his window. The sheep watched his reflection for several hours before crashing through the glass and landing, unconscious, on the floor.

In a similar incident in Pennsylvania in 1988, Kelly Kyle, 17, was at home alone in the living room when she noticed deer in the yard. One suddenly crashed through the living room window and was followed by four others, after which all five proceeded to trash the house. At the time, Kelly's father was out deer hunting.

OCCUPATIONAL HAZARDS

Striking workers at a chemical plant in Cuernavaca, Mexico, announced two demands: a 35 percent wage hike and smaller breasts—for men. About three dozen male workers at the plant, which makes female hormones used in birth control pills, experienced unnatural development of their breasts and, their union leader said, "have faced social problems to a considerable degree." Female workers were unaffected.

○

Safety engineers checking the emergency braking system on a 480-foot mine-shaft elevator in Ashington, England, raised the elevator to the surface and then sent it into a free fall four times before discovering that two miners were trapped inside. "I never want to get back into a pit cage as long as I live," said Mark Hetherington, one of the men bounced up and down inside the elevator for two hours.

After Jimmy Carter's friendship for the Polish people was misinterpreted as lust, translators came under greater pressure to avoid lost meanings. At a news conference after a team handball match between West Germany and the United States, a reporter speaking German asked U.S. coach Javier Cuesta how long his team had trained and how hard.

Cuesta replied in English: "We've been together since January, training five days a week, four or five hours a day."

He then turned the microphone over to the translator, who said, "We've been together since January, training five days a week, four to five hours a day"—also in perfect English.

O

Air Force Lt. Col. Charles "Mike" Johnson, 40, was one of three people killed when two small planes collided near Des Arc, Arkansas, while their occupants were waving at people below. Johnson, who was piloting one of the planes, was chief of flying safety for his unit.

O

Alice E. Rossell, 56, of Guerneville, California, was celebrating winning the football pool at the apple cannery where she worked by passing out doughnuts when her clothing snagged on a machine and she was pulled to her death before horrified co-workers, who were unable to rescue her.

O

Denver barber Bobbie D. Willis, 46, was shot to death by a customer who didn't like his haircut. Another barber said the assailant, who had a 2½-inch scar shaped like a half moon on the back of his head, came in with a picture showing Willis how he wanted his hair cut and that during and after the haircut he "kept screaming that he messed up his hair, that he'd cut him bald." The man returned to the shop three hours later and shot Willis, who was on the phone to the police complaining about the enraged customer lurking outside.

○

Bob Holt, 20, hired to dress up as a duck to advertise a Seattle radio station, was attacked on a downtown street by a man who spun him around by one wing, pulled off his duck bill, and beat him over the head with it, then ran off. "I didn't speak to him," Holt said. "I didn't flap my wings. I didn't do anything like that."

○

At a concert in Nottingham, England, by the Polish Radio Symphony Orchestra, pianist Wladyslaw Kedra was performing a solo when a piece of wood fell off and clattered to the floor. Kedra stopped abruptly, then tried a foot pedal. It wouldn't work, so he walked off, followed by conductor Jan Krenz.

On came piano tuner John Spaiding and two assistants, who pushed and hammered for 10 minutes. Then Kedra and Krenz returned, and the concert resumed. The piano began falling apart again, but Kedra carried on. At the end of his performance, Kedra bowed while the piano was pushed to one side as the audience cheered, and the whole pedal mechanism fell out and tumbled in a heap on the platform.

○

Loren Tobia, news director for WSAZ-TV in Charleston, West Virginia, was covering a news conference by H. John Rogers, a candidate for the U.S. Senate who had just been detained four days at a Wheeling mental health center for spitting in the face of a police chief. Following his speech, which he interrupted to berate another TV reporter for not paying attention, Rogers asked if there were any serious questions. Tobia asked the first one: "Do you think your recent stay in a mental institution will hurt your candidacy?"

Rogers got up from the couch where he was sitting and strode over to Tobia. "Was that a serious question?" he asked, then punched Tobia in the face.

WRONG ARM OF THE LAW

FBI agents who thought they spotted murder suspect Robert Lee Swofford at his father's funeral in Petersburg, Virginia, moved in to block the funeral procession. They ordered the immediate family out of their limousine at gunpoint only to discover the man in question was Swofford's stepbrother.

"You have to do the best you can in a nasty situation," said FBI spokesman Jim Watters. "My condolences go out to the family."

○

In Atlanta, a daring thief stole $8,900 worth of cameras and accessories from an exhibit booth at a convention for crime-detection experts. His getaway was delayed by having to pretend to be a salesman and give a 45-minute sales pitch to a security guard who had seen him walking off with the goods.

When Roy Glenn, 18, appeared before County Judge Don Meyers in Salida, Colorado, to protest the ticket given him by a state game and fish officer for having thrown an empty beverage can on the ground at a state fish hatchery, Glenn pointed out that after the officer had written the ticket, he tore off some ticket stubs and threw them on the ground. The judge, noting that the officer was as guilty as the youth, dismissed the case.

○

Police in Tulsa, responding to an emergency call that a man was holding a woman at knifepoint, surrounded the wrong house. The man was in the house next door. He tried several times to surrender, but the police, thinking he was just a nosy neighbor, kept ordering him back inside. After about an hour, a newspaper photographer who lived nearby alerted police to their mistake.

○

Leonard Ostrow, a building contractor in Placer County, California, sued the FBI for poor paint jobs by its agents. The agents were working undercover as painters while investigating allegations of corruption in the construction industry. Ostrow was not a target of the investigation, but he hired the FBI painters to paint four custom homes he was building. In his suit, which was settled out of court, he charged that the FBI had done such a poor job painting the homes that he refused to pay them and had to have the job done over, holding up the sale of the homes.

○

In Florida, Dade County and Jacksonville officials discovered that their new $34 million jail was being built with 195 cells—but no cell doors. Michael Berg, city-county director of jails and prisons, said he wasn't sure how the oversight occurred but that there was money to pay the extra $1.5 million to have the doors added.

And at the Ontario County Jail in Canandaigua, New York, installation of new cell doors was halted when officials discovered the bars were too far apart and prisoners could slip through them.

○

Undercover police in Pompano Beach, Florida, arranged to sell two pounds of cocaine. The buyers turned out to be undercover officers from the Fort Lauderdale police.

○

Police in Van Nuys, California, arrested Dennis John Alston on charges of forging checks, then released him when he posted bail with a $1,500 cashier's check. It turned out to be a forgery.

○

Tommy Cribbs, the sheriff of Dyer County, Tennessee, was arrested in Van Buren, Missouri, after police noticed his car in the parking lot of a local motel. A car of that description had been used in the theft of two sheep from a nearby farm. Officers who were questioning people at the motel were led to Cribbs after a sheep was thrown from the window of his room.

○

Police in Sydney Mines, Nova Scotia, raided their own Christmas party for not having a license to serve liquor.

Within a three-month period in 1989, guards at two prisons fell for the old soap-gun trick. In Crown Point, Indiana, convicted burglar Robert Edward Gregory, 25, used a pistol carved from a bar of soap to escape from the Lake County Jail, then used it to steal a car. He was caught an hour later. And in Perry, Georgia, Roy Kenneth Sanford, 23, serving time for armed robbery and kidnapping, escaped after pulling a soap pistol on three prison guards. He was arrested the next day.

ODD ENDINGS

A car being driven by Joseph Briggs, 60, of West Philadelphia slammed into two utility poles, plunged down a 20-foot embankment, and crashed through a fence. Briggs walked away from his demolished car without a scratch—only to be struck and killed by a passing truck.

○

Diane Sims, 25, of Niagara Falls, New York, who was admitted to a hospital for minor surgery, died, according to Niagara County Coroner James Joyce, when her nightgown accidentally caught on a sink in her private room and strangled her.

○

Peter Aiello, 21, of McHenry, Illinois, who never gave up playing cowboys and Indians, died after a fire engulfed a tepee he had been occupying to recreate the lifestyle of his heroes. The blaze was discovered by a friend in a nearby tepee.

Patrick Viola, 22, died at an outdoor party in Albany, New York, when someone placed a nearly empty keg in a bonfire. The remaining liquid began to boil, causing steam and pressure to build until the keg blew up, and a flying piece of metal entered the right side of Viola's neck and severed his spinal cord.

○

Eleanor Berry, 70, died as she lay in the bedroom of her Long Island home when a huge pile of books, newspapers, and press clippings fell on her and the weight of the papers muffled her cries for help. Police had to use an ax to smash open the bedroom door because the collapsed pile blocked their entry. They said the entire house was filled with towers of books, newspapers, shopping bags, and assorted papers.

○

Rabsary Gutierrez, 16, died after crashing through a skylight while taking pictures for her high school yearbook in Hialeah, Florida.

○

In Sabac, Yugoslavia, a 57-year-old woman was killed when she was hit by a 15-year-old boy who plunged from a seventh-floor balcony. The boy survived with only a broken leg.

○

Aniceto Villarta, 35, was fishing with friends in the town of Alcoy on the island of Cebu in the Philippines. He caught a fish and used his teeth to unhook his catch, but the fish, still alive, wiggled into his throat and suffocated him.

In Hadley, New York, 28-year-old Bruce Jay Weiss became angry when the family cat urinated on the floor. He took a .16-gauge shotgun from a closet, loaded a round, and then tried to swat the cat with the butt end. It discharged, fatally shooting Weiss in the throat.

○

Frances Farthing, 80, was killed while waiting for a bus in Poulton-le-Fylde, England, when a wheel came off a car that was being towed, rolled across the road, and struck her.

○

Angelo Thurman, 22, was waiting at a Chicago subway station with friends when he announced he would show them how to tell if a train was coming. He jumped from the platform, placed his ear to the electrified third rail, and was electrocuted.

○

Mexicans Enrique Simental and Lupe Cardenas were drinking with friends and playing Russian roulette at an apartment in Reno. They decided to stand side by side and press their heads together. One pulled the trigger, the gun fired, and the bullet went through their heads, killing both men.

○

Don Terrell Henderson of Texas City, Texas, was leaning out of a car smashing mailboxes on posts with a baseball bat, when his head caught on one of the mailboxes and jerked him out of the car, killing him. Another mailbox victim was a 6-year-old boy in Bethesda, Maryland. A mail-collection box with missing bolts toppled onto him, killing him under its weight. The next day, Postal Service investigators found that 250 of the 6,000 mailboxes in the area had loose or missing bolts.

○

In Los Angeles, a burglar who stayed to watch television and eat a snack at a home he broke into died from toxic fumes being used to fumigate the house.

EVEN *WE* DIDN'T BELIEVE THESE

A man in Ypsilanti, Michigan, gave up his wallet (containing $23) to a mugger but claimed later he did not realize that the mugger had also shot him until he started getting head-aches three days later. He said he didn't see a gun and didn't hear a bang, but doctors removed a bullet from behind his left ear.

○

A man robbed Wayne's Bait and Supply in Osage Beach, Missouri, and, to prevent the people inside (the owner, his wife, his daughter, and a customer) from chasing him, he glued them to the floor with Super Glue.

○

A legless Eddie "Eddie the Monkey Man" Bernstein died in Pensacola, Florida, in his sleep. He was a notorious beggar with a pet monkey in Washington, D.C., but the *Washington Post* reported that he left an estate of $691,716. During the spring and summer, he begged out of a foul-smelling apartment in Washington, but he wintered in Florida, where he led a life of leisure and read the *Wall Street Journal* daily.

○

A vintage 1946 airplane that a Lorraine, New York, man had spent four years rebuilding took off by itself in 1987 from a local airstrip when the man accidentally left the throttle open while cranking it. When the plane crashed ten miles away, his wife told reporters that in thirty years of marriage, this was one of the very few times she had seen her husband cry.

○

A gunman entered a dormitory of the Pompano Beach (Florida) Community Correctional Center and robbed an inmate serving an armed-robbery sentence, leaving with a stereo, a radio, a TV set, and other items. Said the prison superintendent, "If you're not safe in prison from armed robbery, where are you safe?"

○

Bullets fired at close range have failed to injure their targets seriously for the following reasons:

- bounced off the button on a 16-year-old boy's jeans (St. Paul, Minnesota)

- bounced off his zipper (Angel Santana, 51, fending off a robbery attempt in New York City)

- bounced off a golf ball in his pocket (golf-course robbery victim in Memphis)

- lodged in the barrel of the victim's own drawn gun (federal drug agent Carlos Montalvo, Hialeah, Florida)

- bounced off her false teeth (Broken Bow, Oklahoma)

- "bounced off" the skull of mobster Joe "Tokyo Joe" Eto, victim of a hit man (Chicago, 1983)

- And finally, a murder-suicide pact in West Vancouver, between a man, 89, and his wife, 92, failed because the gun he used hadn't been fired in at least fifty years. His shot to the wife's head ricocheted off a hair curler, causing only a flesh wound. When he put the gun to his own head and pulled the trigger, the bullet lodged in his ear, dazing the man.

LISTS

Not Dead Yet

Assumed dead, the following people woke up just in time: 82-year-old Helen Francoeur of Massachusetts (funeral home workers saw her body move and she was hospitalized for dehydration); Charles Herrell, 56, of West Virginia, woke up inside a plastic body bag at a funeral home in 1980, a victim of hypoglycemia; 87-year-old Carrie Stringfellow, who moaned while an Ohio undertaker prepared to embalm her in 1989; narcoleptic Frederick Kerr, 37, in New Zealand, who also awoke on the embalming table and punched mortician George Gossett in the face in 1986; and Jerry Middleswart, pronounced dead from a 7,600-volt charge of electricity, mysteriously revived forty minutes later (but died again soon after, this time for real).

○

Travelers in the Twilight Zone

The following elderly people got lost while driving in their cars: 76-year-old Frank Collier of Centerville, Alabama, on his way to the dentist in 1988 (instead of driving 74 miles to Pell City, he drove 560 miles to Muncie, Indiana); Floridian Joseph Stophel, 79, from Dunedin, who, while driving in Georgia, was listed as missing for a week as he drove through Indiana, Tennessee, and Kentucky; and Russell and Ruby Grafton, both in their seventies, of Carman, Illinois, who turned a 40-mile trip home into a 4,000-mile journey over nine days, traveling possibly as far north as Chicago and as far south as Paducah, Kentucky, passing through Missouri and possibly Indiana.

○

Trapped

In a 1988 attempt to crawl through a window into his father's house, Rocky Benedetto, 31, of Pittsford, New York, got trapped in a 9-inch opening and suffocated. Also that year, two men in California were trapped in chimneys: Rodolpho Mohoro, because he was locked out of a relative's house one night, and Hector Medina, allegedly as he attempted a burglary. Those stuck in chimneys in 1989 included a man in Jones, Oklahoma, who was trying to get into his estranged wife's home; an alleged burglar who got stuck in the chimney of a New York restaurant and died from suffocation; Keeno Exum, 27, who got stuck and cooked to death in a Delaware church chimney; and 31-year-old James Edward Burgess of St. Petersburg, Florida, who got stuck in a chimney in an alleged burglary attempt of a doctor's office (police advised him of his rights as rescue workers tried to free him). Those trapped for too long in chimneys: the skeleton of an alleged burglar at a West Baltimore furniture warehouse found in a chimney that hadn't been cleaned for three years; and Ronald Blount, a New Haven, Connecticut, roofer who was last seen entering the bathroom in his rooming house in March 1983 and was found in the building's chimney years later (for no known reason he apparently crawled out the bathroom window onto the roof and got in).

Trapped through no fault of her own in 1989 was Pamela Cohen, 26, of Bayshore, New York, who just happened to be sitting in her car when a truck carrying hot asphalt overturned and almost completely sealed her inside. Rescuers had to dig her a breathing passage and were assured she was alive by her honking car horn.

○

Low-Speed Chases

The year 1989 saw at least three low-speed chases: Californian Brett T. Barish, 29, led two patrol cars and a police helicopter on a four-hour chase through four counties at speeds that never rose above the 55 mph speed limit; a thief in Bellefonte, Pennsylvania, drove a tractor at its top speed of 15 mph as police chased him for two miles, escaping when he drove into a field and ran away; and an 8-year-old near Roanoke, Virginia, who took his mother's car (while she was speaking to his school principal) and led police on a 12-mile chase.

Some older low-speed chases: Police Chief Dennis Chance said that three alleged bank robbers in Berlin, New Jersey, were easily apprehended after a 3-mph chase—their 17-year-old Cadillac got stuck in first gear. Also, in Arizona, 34-year-old Sharon Walker chased a flasher about 30 yards on her horse— he rode a bicycle in a getaway attempt—and held him for police by riding around him in a tight circle.

○

Joyrides

Joyriding knows no age:

Youngsters behind the wheel in the late 1980s included: a 3-year-old in Amsterdam who climbed into a parked van and drove it into five market stalls, slightly injuring six; a 6-year-old in Tappan, New York, who, headed for his father's house, took his grandmother's Chrysler, and drove five miles before being overtaken; a 7-year-old from Amarillo, Texas, who took his parents' 1981 Buick and tried to drive his 3-year-old sister and 8-year-old friend to his grandfather's in Oklahoma but hit a road construction barrel and was stopped (he took the car out again a week later); a 12-year-old who stole a car with a 15-year-old in Utah and led police on a 95-mph chase; another 12-year-old who took her mom's car from Long Eddy, New York, and headed for her father's in Berkeley Heights, making it 100 miles before being stopped; and a 13-year-old who stole his parents' car in Dallas twice in one day—the second time at knifepoint on their way home from jail.

Or species:

In Norwalk, Connecticut, Ebony, an 8-month-old German shepherd, pushed her owner, Joseph Vellone, out of his car at a red light when he opened his door to spit. She then sat in the front seat alone while the car rolled through an intersection and into a building.

Or vehicle of choice:

In 1989 three gendarmes in Mimizan-Plage, France, took their dates aboard a police helicopter for a nighttime joyride and crashed into the Atlantic, killing all six. That same year, William Stacy, 24, who didn't know how to fly, took a single-engine airplane for a ride from an Arlington, Texas, airport and crashed, killing himself. Stacy had been arrested two years earlier for taking another plane for a joyride. In Los Angeles Harbor, Roy Bennett and Danny Andrews, both 28, along with a 15-year-old companion, took the Catalina Island ferry for a joyride but had to be rescued after the engine overheated and the ferry burned.

UNCATE-GORICALLY WEIRD

Attempting to demonstrate that he was physically fit to be president, George Wallace aired television commercials during the 1976 election campaign that showed him catching a football in his wheelchair. "I'm not trying to compare myself with Roosevelt," Wallace said later, "but he couldn't walk either."

○

A construction company in Saipan, Northern Marianas, placed a notice in the local newspaper after one of its flashing amber warning lights was stolen from a road construction site on March 28, 1984. Noting that the lights were necessary to warn motorists of the excavation so they could avoid an accident, the company said it was removing "the remaining warning lights and we are not going to install them again unless we are sure that they will not be stolen."

Officials at the Houston Zoo admitted that their coral snake was a rubber imitation. "We had live snakes in the exhibit, but they didn't do well," said curator John Donaho. "They tend to die."

○

Robert Kropinski of Philadelphia sued Transcendental Meditation groups where he spent eleven years as a student and teacher, claiming he suffered psychological disorders as a result of never achieving the "perfect state of life" the group promised. The 36-year-old real-estate manager said, for example, that the groups had told him he would be taught to "fly" through self-levitation, but all he learned to do was "hop with the legs folded in the lotus position."

○

After Gary Starr, 47, was convicted of murdering his 20-year-old daughter, he asked a judge to confirm his death sentence as soon as possible so he could be transferred from an area of the State Correctional Institution of Pittsburgh where television sets are prohibited to death row, where he could watch TV in his cell.

○

Villagers in East Java, faced with a plague of rats ravaging their rice fields in 1985, began catching live rats, sewing up their anuses with strands of plastic string, then releasing them. Crazed by being unable to defecate, the rodents would turn on their fellow rats and bite them to death before dying themselves, usually in about three days. Villagers in Lumajang claimed to have killed 60,000 rats this way in just three weeks.

A fight erupted on the floor of a world peace conference in Copenhagen in 1986 when protestors took the stage and accused the Soviet KGB of being behind the conference, causing other demonstrators to accuse the protestors of being CIA dupes.

And in London in 1980, a group of women demonstrating against violence smashed a window at a movie theater, then fought with police who intervened to restore order, injuring five of the officers.

○

Henry Leroy Hensen, 34, despite being handcuffed and in leg irons, skipped away from Patton State Mental Hospital in San Bernardino County, California, using a jumprope. He escaped several days before a preliminary court session on his request for a sanity hearing. His attorney explained to the judge that Hensen made the jumprope at a hospital macramé class.

○

Schenectady, New York, police sergeant Rudy Basha described the scene at 64-year-old Iva Fletcher's house in 1979 as "unbelievable but true." Police called to the house found an ankle-deep swarm of cockroaches stretching from the door to the street and into the trees. The officers estimated the number of roaches at "hundreds of thousands" but an exterminator called to the scene said it was "definitely in the millions." Fletcher was found inside the house along with two dozen dogs, fifteen cats, two mice, and a parrot. All had cockroach and flea bites. The ambulance that took Fletcher to the hospital, as well as an animal shelter van and four police vehicles, all had to be fumigated. One policeman was reportedly covered with cockroaches as he got out of his patrol car. The walls inside the house were described as "so full that [the cockroaches] had nowhere else to go."

West German police arrested an Austrian vagrant for cooking onion soup over Berlin's "eternal flame." He had been warned against cooking there in an earlier incident when he tried to make dumplings.

○

Responding to a call from concerned neighbors in 1982, Newport Beach, California, police found the body of Grace Lee, 78, buried under tons of garbage stored inside her home. City workers removed five tons of rotting food, trash, and debris before Lee's body was uncovered. "There was a minimum of three feet of trash throughout the house and drifts as high as six feet in places. She apparently walked on top of the trash to get from one room to another," said officer Tim Newman. "There wasn't even a functioning toilet. . . . There wasn't a bed or chair that wasn't covered by trash. We eventually found couches and carpeting at the bottom of the pile."

○

In 1987 Bill Bartlett, associate national album director for Capitol Records, sued Walter Lee, Capitol's senior vice-president of promotion and marketing, charging that Lee shocked him with an electric cattle prod on several occasions in the office. In one alleged incident, when Bartlett went to Lee's office to discuss a promotional trip, Lee allegedly shocked him with the prod in the presence of company president Don Zimmermann, saying, "If you don't get airplay on this trip, you'll get more of this." Bartlett's complaint charged that Zimmermann "laughed in agreement."

APPENDIX: A Few Notes on Weirdology

"Weird"

Weird, adj. 1: of, relating to, or caused by witchcraft or the supernatural: MAGICAL 2: of strange or extraordinary character: ODD, FANTASTIC. syn: WEIRD, EERIE, UNCANNY. shared meaning element: mysteriously strange or fantastic [Webster's New Collegiate Dictionary]

Most of the stories in *News of the Weird* are funny, but "funny" is only a small subset of "weird." Occasional exchanges with our readers run something like this:

READER: Hey, what about that chicken story, where the farmer had sex with the chicken, then tied her up with little leather legcuffs. I suppose you think that's *funny*. I suppose you think mass murder is *funny*. I'll bet you think husbands' beating up their wives is *funny*.

THE AUTHORS: Nope. In fact, we've often included such stories *because* they *aren't funny*. We were shocked by them. They make us shake our heads in disbelief.

READER: Well, if you feel that way, you shouldn't be printing that stuff. You're just going to encourage all those psychos. No telling what kind of things they'll be doing.

THE AUTHORS: Maybe, but the research doesn't show that. It is possible that a very few potential psychos will gain confidence in their pathologies by reading news of what other people have done. But murders and mutilations and animal abuse are such grotesque behaviors that they can hardly be learned from reading books. There are very weird people in this country and on this planet.

READER: Even if you're right, even if you just make a small contribution to the problem, that's enough to get you to stop. You shouldn't be publicizing these stories if even one innocent person becomes the victim of a "copycat" weirdo.

THE AUTHORS: But there is at least as much evidence that calling a problem to attention by ridicule might prevent or lessen the incidence of the problem. Violence against humans and abuse of animals are strange, bizarre, and unacceptable occurrences. We believe that if people know how often these things occur, they will be more—not less—sensitive to them.

READER: So you're not going to restrain yourselves?

THE AUTHORS: First of all, everything we print has been published somewhere else before—in a major newspaper or magazine. It's not like we're revealing some secret. Second, we have exercised restraint. There is no gratuitous news of violence—without some larger lesson or irony. But unless someone offers evidence—and not just speculation —that copycat tragedy outweighs the sensitization that comes with publicity about the problem, we'll keep right on going.

READER: Well, just what kind of stuff is it that you think isn't funny and is kinda scary?

THE AUTHORS: Well, how about this: Here's a partial list of reasons we've collected, from clippings, of why human beings have killed other human beings recently. Understand the tragedy here: Human beings. *Dead.* Killed by other human beings. Killed by advanced mammals with high orders of intelligence. And *these* are the reasons.

- which country, Korea or China, has the more pleasant lifestyle
- why he should pick up toys around the house
- obnoxiously switched TV channels
- whether he and his wife should take a honeymoon cruise
- refused to lend him her car
- spare the mother the anguish of finding out that her daughter was murdered because she had refused to lend out her car
- quality of the biscuits they were eating
- child failed to get past "g" while reciting the alphabet
- council members wouldn't do anything about his backed-up sewer

- played a stereo too loud

- used his driveway to turn her car around in

- objected to his friend's being robbed of his Popsicle

- criticized him for spitting into an ashtray at their nursing home

- mayor turned him down for a car-washing license

- whether the lights should be on in their room at a nursing home

- made a bad call during a playground basketball game he was officiating

- cursed during dinner at a friend's house

- ate the hamburger and pork and beans she had set out on the counter for her daughter's meal

- didn't bathe properly

- parked in his condominium parking space

- where son and daughter-in-law would spend Father's Day

- failed to kneel properly when praying

- interrupted his meal and television-watching

- complained that there were too many nails in the street behind his store

- refused to lend him money to play video games

- too slow making a left turn at a traffic light

- made derogatory remarks about Jesus Christ

- whether there would be enough meat loaf for everyone at a family dinner

- whose turn it was to drive the car

- refused to be convinced that topless sunbathing is immoral

- upset over customer's complaint about poor service
- didn't wait on him when it was his turn to be waited on
- cut in front of him in the popcorn line at a theater
- thought she was responsible when their dog urinated on him
- which of two men was better educated
- interrupted a game of Pac Man
- professor gave him a low grade
- woman paid him $100 to kill her husband
- thought (erroneously) that the gold crowns in their father's teeth bore the numbers of Swiss bank accounts
- two-year-old boy paddled for two hours straight in a "test of wills" between him and his parents and their minister
- dented his $70,000 Ferrari
- objected to grass-trimming by neighbor
- shouted at murderer (who was driving by) to slow down
- wanted to get an advance look at his military exam questions for the next day
- came to the aid of a stray cat the murderer was abusing
- gave her nothing for Christmas and then complained about the gift she had given him
- chef refused to serve him chicken on Christmas Eve
- had a different strategy for trimming the Christmas tree
- whereabouts of a missing shirt
- placed newspaper and mustard on the wrong side of the plate when setting the dinner table

- meant only to wound her but couldn't because shooting at her legs would have endangered the family dog

- feared parents would make him withdraw from school because of low grades

- her goats had wandered onto his property

- interrupted his Bible-reading session

- "tired of [her month-old baby]"

- not doing enough housework

- accidentally disconnected a telephone call

- called him "señorita"

- mistakenly believed he was the same man who drugged his communion wine ten years earlier

- innocently made the hand gesture of a rival gang

- ownership of various items (tamale, Indian head penny, *Playboy* centerfolds, candy bar, pork chop, salami, hot dog, baseball cards, designer sweatpants, frozen fish)

Aren't you as frightened as we are?

THE STUDY OF STRANGENESS

At this point in our careers, almost no weird news item gets past us, but we're still unable to demystify all the bizarreness that arrives at our mailbox. We're not sure, for example, whether the end of the century has brought us more strangeness or just more data to ponder.

Surely, there is a synchronistic effect at work. One month you see a reference to "train surfing" in Brazil. Within a week you learn of a new sport of "car surfing" at U.S. high schools and then discover the *years-old* pastime of "elevator surfing" in the high-rise dormitories of U.S. universities.

A few years ago, an incident of purposive (nonvandalistic) rock-tossing from a freeway overpass occurred in New York, but was not widely reported. Several months later, a similar incident occurred in Illinois. It is not obvious to us that the kind of Illinois resident who believes it is a good idea to drop concrete chunks onto passing cars read about the previous incident in the Metro section of the *New York Times*.

After years of sifting through data like these, one gets the chilling feeling that "someone" is trying to tell us "something." But our only recourse is to continue to collect the data. Ask anyone who collects this stuff: Not one of us has any idea what it all means. Weird news must pass as its own reward.

The most serious weirdologists refer to themselves as Forteans, after Charles Hoy Fort (1874–1932), a brilliant American writer obsessed with recording the unexplained and who delighted in taunting establishment science with its inability to explain his data. His "data" were voluminous clippings from established newspapers around the world. Modern-day Forteans can present an astounding record of things seen in the sky, strange creatures that haunt all our back woods, and many other unexplained phenomena.

Forteans' field today is littered with questions of no small controversy: from the extraordinary UFO sightings in Gulf Breeze, Florida (which have proved divisive within the "UFO community"), to the strange circles appearing in wheatfields all over England, to the debate over whether Bigfoot is flesh and blood or something more ephemeral, to Richard Hoagland's research into strange formations on Mars discovered in the 1976 Viking space probe photos, to the source of mystery helicopters that seem to be tailing various researchers as they make their rounds. Those represent just the more well-known tip of a very strange iceberg.

We are not classic Forteans, but we have managed to meet some talented Forteans: author Loren Coleman; Mark Chorvinsky, the editor of *Strange* magazine; Ray Manners, the editor of *Info*, the International Fortean Organization's journal of "science and the unknown"; and Ray Nelke, founder of Collectors of Unusual Data—International (COUD-I). Our work has profited from our association with these and other members of the formidable network of American Forteans.

However, we find ourselves on a different track from the Forteans'. Sure, we want to read the report about the giant batlike creature seen in some remote part of the country (and, please, if you have such a clip, kindly send it to us). But we're more interested in people who *worship* giant batlike creatures, or who want to *marry* giant batlike creatures. That is, we view ourselves mainly as recorders of human behavior. Why did the guys on the overpass think it was a good idea to drop concrete chunks on passing cars? Better still, why is there an entire village of people in India that, every year, stops what it's doing and spends the next twenty-four hours throwing rocks at each other attempting to kill or maim as many people as possible (and then, after twenty-four hours, ceases fire, nurses the wounded, and buries the dead)?

At the very least, the study of strangeness gives us all faith that we're personally not so peculiar. Our work gives us the opportunity to tell ourselves, "I thought I was a little strange, but then again, I never stood on the front lawn wrapped in aluminum foil to ward off gamma rays." And even if you did do that, there's *still* something in our books to make you feel better about yourself. Maybe *that's* the legacy of weirdology.

THE SUPERMARKET TABLOIDS

A rare, but puzzling reaction to *News of the Weird* is that it is too incredible to be true, that it smacks of the supermarket tabloids (which are the professional wrestling of journalism). If that reaction means that weird news is entertaining, good. If that reaction means that people suspect our weird news is fake, bad.

To us, facts are the whole point. With our work, we've constructed a meadow in which all who romp there know that everything they read will be true. Upon entering our meadow, the reader can rest assured that his or her reaction to a story (be it laughter or chills) is freed of the guilt one may feel while standing in the supermarket check-out line. After all, it's a *real* reaction to a *real* story.

That is not to say that we don't like the tabloids. (We're just at a loss to understand why they *bother* making anything up, what with all the reality in the world.) One reason is that there is much *true* news in the tabloids (even though we don't rely on those stories for our work). They get most of their stories from daily newspapers. A couple of years ago, the managing editor of *Weekly World News* told the Florida Press Club that his paper gets 275 daily papers from around the country and 55 foreign dailies—and pays four people to do nothing but scan them for weird news. (According to a newspaper report of the editor's speech, he also explained some tricks of his trade, such as making even the silliest story seem at least slightly credible by placing it next to a strange-but-true story that might be recalled by some readers from their own daily newspaper, hoping the credibility will rub off.)

But you won't see us sensationalize reality. No exclamation points or colorful adjectives. No tipping off the reader on how he or she is "supposed" to be entertained by the story. Not even any cute headlines to introduce the stories. Just pure reality. Read it and weep.

THE CASE OF THE ELUSIVE COCKROACH

The major occupational hazard for us weirdologists is the risk of taking seriously a fictional story. Ordinarily, it is enough if we rely on the major media as our sources—but not always. More than once, mainstream journalists have been caught up with so-called "urban legends"—stories that are dressed up as true with the professional patois of news but are actually yarns that have been making the rounds for years.

We are fans of the leading chronicler of urban legends, Professor Jan Harold Brunvand, of the University of Utah, and we have used his work to help us screen them out as they find their way to us. That requires being especially vigilant of items that appear too good to be true.

The most recent urban legend incident in which fiction made its rounds among the mainstream media was the notorious "elusive cockroach" story filed on August 25, 1988, by a reporter for the *Jerusalem Post* and then distributed worldwide by Reuters.

According to the story, a Tel Aviv housewife was frightened by seeing a cockroach in her living room. To exterminate it, she stepped on it, threw it in a toilet, and sprayed a whole can of insecticide on it when it initially refused to die. When her husband came home from work and sat on the toilet, he innocently lit a cigarette and threw the butt in the bowl, where the insecticide fumes ignited, "seriously burning his sensitive parts," according to the *Post*. Paramedics taking him to an ambulance on a stretcher inquired how the injury occurred, began laughing uncontrollably at the story, and dropped the body off the stretcher, causing him to suffer "further injury."

Among the news outlets that ran the story uncritically were the *Los Angeles Times,* the *Houston Post,* the *Washington Times,* the *San Francisco Chronicle,* the *Philadelphia Inquirer,* the *Boston Globe,* the *Orlando Sentinel*, and WUSA-TV in Washington, D.C.

Your faithful authors were not tempted to believe the story, however, for we had seen it before—several times. Three such incidents were:

Akron, Ohio, carried in the *Akron Beacon Journal* (around 1974)

Belle Glade, Florida, carried in the *Palm Beach Post Times* (around 1975)

Cleveland, carried in the *Cleveland Press* (around 1980)

Sure enough, five days after the story ran, the *Post* retracted it, and so did Reuters, with apologies to their readers.

But not everyone heard about the retraction. Several weeks later, that supermarket tabloid *par excellence*, *Weekly World News*, carried its report of the story. Not only did the story contain more detail than did the original *Jerusalem Post* story, but the article was replete with purported direct quotes from the housewife, her husband, and the paramedic who dropped the body. Ah! *That's* journalism!

SOURCES

Agence France-Press

The Alabama Journal (Montgomery)

The American Journal of Forensic Medicine and Pathology

The American Lawyer

The American Spectator

The Arizona Daily Star (Tucson)

Asbury Park Press (New Jersey)

The Asheville Citizen (North Carolina)

Associated Press

The Athens Messenger (Ohio)

The Atlantic

Australian Medical Journal

Aviation Week & Space Technology

The Beaumont Enterprise (Texas)

Billboard

Black Mountain News (North Carolina)

The Boston Globe

Chicago Tribune

The Courier-Journal (Louisville, Kentucky)

Daily Telegraph (London, England)

The Dallas Morning News

Dayton Daily News (Ohio)

The Des Moines Register (Iowa)
Detroit Free Press
Deutsche-Presse-Agentur
The Evening Sun (Baltimore, Maryland)
Freethought Today
Gainesville Sun (Florida)
Gannett News Service
Goleta Sun (California)
Houston Chronicle
Idaho State Journal (Pocatello)
The Independent (London, England)
The Journal of Commerce
Laredo Morning Times (Texas)
Leaders
Lexington Herald-Leader (Kentucky)
Los Angeles Herald Examiner
Los Angeles Times
The Miami Herald
The Milwaukee Journal
Milwaukee Sentinel
Monday Magazine (Victoria, British Columbia)
National Council Against Health Fraud newsletter
National Law Journal
New Straits Times (Malaysia)
New Times
New York Daily News
New York Post
The New York Times
News-Pilot (San Pedro, California)
The Olympian (Olympia, Washington)
Parade
The Philadelphia Inquirer

Physician's Weekly
The Pittsburgh Press
The Plain Dealer (Cleveland, Ohio)
The Post-Standard (Syracuse, New York)
Press-Telegram (Long Beach, California)
The Progressive
The Record (Bergen County, New Jersey)
Reuters
Richmond Times-Dispatch
St. Louis Post-Dispatch
St. Paul Pioneer Press & Dispatch (Minnesota)
St. Petersburg Times
Salt Lake Tribune (Salt Lake City, Utah)
San Francisco Chronicle
San Francisco Examiner
San José Mercury News (California)
Santa Barbara News-Press
Seattle Post-Intelligencer
The Seattle Times
The Star-Ledger (Newark, New Jersey)
The State (Columbia, South Carolina)
The Sun (Baltimore)
Syracuse Herald American (New York)
Syracuse Herald-Journal (New York)
Syracuse New Times (New York)
Tampa Tribune
The Toronto Star
The Toronto Sun
The Tribune (Oakland, California)
The Tuscaloosa News (Alabama)
The Virginian-Pilot (Norfolk, Virginia)
The Wall Street Journal

The Washington Monthly
The Washington Post
The Washington Star
The Washington Times
The Washingtonian
Western Morning News (Plymouth, England)
Wisconsin State Journal (Madison)
World Press Review
United Press International
USA Today
USA Weekend